SERIES

MARQUEE

MICROSOFT®

EXCEL 2002

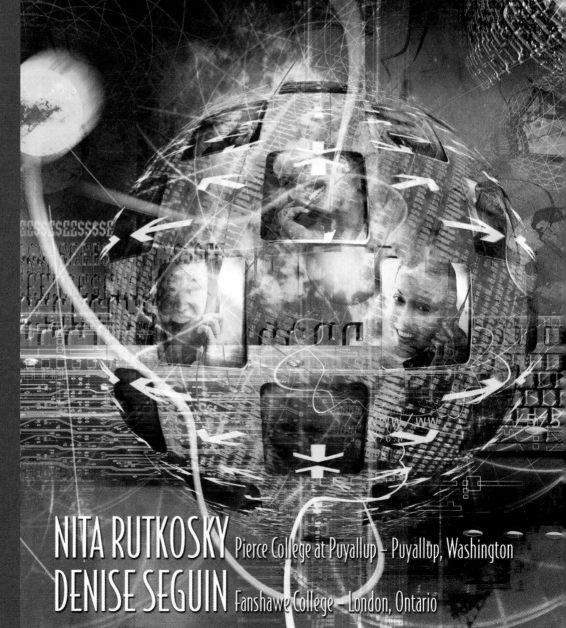

NITA RUTKOSKY Pierce College at Puyallup – Puyallup, Washington

DENISE SEGUIN Fanshawe College – London, Ontario

EMCParadigm

CONTENTS

The Marquee Series Team: Michael Sander, Developmental Editor; Jennifer Wreisner, Senior Designer; Leslie Anderson, Michelle Lewis, and Desktop Solutions, Desktop Production; Desiree Faulkner, Tester; Sharon O'Donnell, Copyeditor; Lynn Reichel, Proofreader; and Nancy Fulton, Indexer.

Publishing Team: George Provol, Publisher; Janice Johnson, Director of Product Development; Tony Galvin, Acquisitions Editor; Lori Landwer, Marketing Manager; Shelley Clubb, Electronic Design and Production Manager.

Acknowledgment: The authors and publisher wish to thank the following reviewer for her technical and academic assistance in testing exercises and assessing instruction: Mary A. Walthall, Ph.D., St. Petersburg College, Clearwater Campus, Clearwater, FL

Library of Congress Cataloging-in-Publication Data
Rutkosky, Nita Hewitt.
Microsoft Excel 2002 / Nita Rutkosky, Denise Seguin.
p.cm. – (Marquee series)
Includes index.
ISBN 0-7638-1467-9 (text) – ISBN 0-7638-1468-7 (text & CD)
1. Microsoft Excel for Windows. 2. Business—Computer programs. 3. Electronic spreadsheets. I. Seguin, Denise. II. Title. III. Series

HF5548.4.M523 R88 2002
055.369—dc21   2001040493

Text + CD: 0-7638-1468-7
Order Number: 05555

© 2002 by Paradigm Publishing Inc.
Published by **EMC**Paradigm   (800) 535-6865
875 Montreal Way   E-mail: educate@emcp.com
St. Paul, MN 55102   Web site: www.emcp.com

Printed in the United States of America   10 9 8 7 6 5 4 3 2

Analyzing Data Using Excel

Microsoft Excel is an application that is used to track, analyze, and chart numeric information such as financial data, statistical values, grades, or any other items that can be established in columns and rows. Once data has been entered in an Excel worksheet, you can create formulas to perform mathematical computations. When these formulas are in place, you can manipulate the values to answer questions or create several scenarios. For example, if you are planning to buy a house, you could enter various house prices, down payment amounts, and interest rates, and use Excel to estimate mortgage payments. In this section you will learn the skills and complete the projects described here.

 Note: Before beginning this section, copy to a floppy disk or other folder the Excel S1 *subfolder from the* Excel *folder on the CD that accompanies this textbook, and then make* Excel S1 *the active folder. Steps on copying a folder, deleting a folder, and making a folder active are on the inside of the back cover of this textbook.*

Skills

- Start Excel and identify features in the Excel window
- Enter labels and values
- Use the fill handle to enter a series
- Enter formulas
- Create a formula using AutoSum
- Copy a relative formula
- Test a worksheet for accuracy
- Apply the Currency format to values
- Right align labels
- Use the online help
- Change the page orientation to landscape
- Preview and print a worksheet
- Save a workbook using Save and Save As
- Close a workbook and exit Excel
- Navigate a large worksheet using the mouse and the keyboard
- Jump to a specific cell using Go To

Projects

 Edit a weekly sales report, create a payroll worksheet, browse an inventory report, and create a condensed quarterly income statement.

 Complete an estimated travel expenses worksheet.

 Prepare a price estimate for costume design and rental.

 Create a projected distribution revenue schedule for a new movie release.

1.1 Completing the Excel Worksheet Cycle

Information is created in Excel in a *worksheet* and is saved in a file called a *workbook*. A workbook can contain several worksheets. Imagine a worksheet as a page with horizontal and vertical lines drawn in a grid representing columns and rows. Data is entered into a *cell*, which is the intersection of a column with a row. Columns are lettered A to Z, AA to AZ, BA to BZ, and so on. The last column in the worksheet is labeled IV. Rows are numbered 1, 2, 3, and so on. A column letter and a row number identify each cell. For example, A1 is the cell address for the intersection of column A with row 1. Each worksheet in Excel contains 256 columns and 65,536 rows.

PROJECT: You have been asked to analyze data in a weekly sales report for The Waterfront Bistro by adding data and viewing the impact of changing a cell used to calculate gross margin.

STEPS

① At the Windows desktop, click the Start button ![Start] on the Taskbar.

This causes a pop-up menu to display.

② Point to *Programs*.

Pointing to an option on the Start pop-up menu that displays with a right-pointing triangle after it causes a cascading side menu to appear.

③ Click *Microsoft Excel*.

Depending on your system configuration, the steps you complete to open Excel may vary.

④ At the Excel screen, identify the various features by comparing your screen with the one shown in Figure E1.1. Depending on your system configuration, your screen may vary slightly. (See Table E1.1 for description of the screen features.)

FIGURE E1.1 The Excel Screen

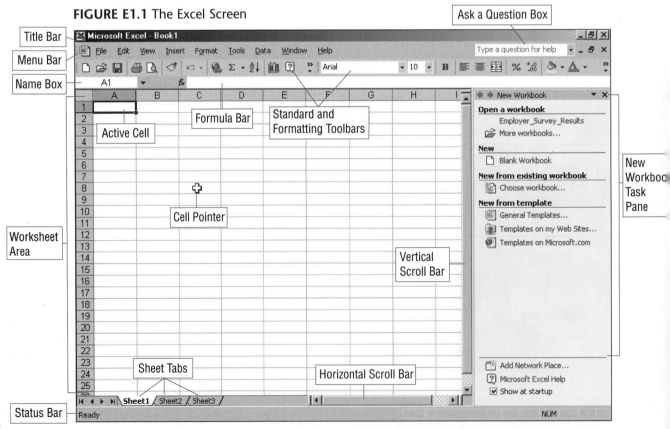

TABLE E1.1 Excel Screen Features

Feature	Description
Title Bar	Displays program name followed by workbook name
Menu Bar	Contains options used to manage and customize workbooks
Ask a Question Box	Used to access help
Standard and Formatting Toolbars	Contain buttons that are shortcuts for popular commands
Name Box	Displays the active cell address
Formula Bar	Displays the active cell entry
Active Cell	Location in the worksheet that will display keyed data or that will be affected by a command
Cell Pointer	Used to select cells
Scroll Bars	Used to navigate the worksheet
Sheet Tab	Identifies the worksheets in the workbook
Worksheet Area	Contains cells used to create the worksheet
Status Bar	Displays information about a command or process
Task Pane	Contains options related to current task being performed

5 Click the Open button 📂 on the Standard toolbar.

6 Make sure the *Excel S1* folder on your disk is the active folder.

> To change to a different drive, click the down-pointing triangle to the right of the Look in text box and then select the correct drive from the drop-down list.

7 Double-click *WB Weekly Sales*.

> This workbook contains one worksheet with sales for The Waterfront Bistro for the week ended September 27, 2003. The formulas to sum the sales have already been created. Notice some of the cells in the column labeled *Saturday* are empty. You will enter these values in steps 10 through 13.

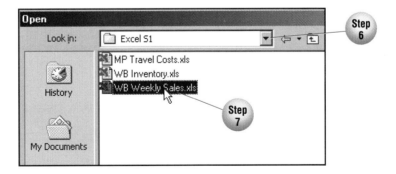

8 Click File and then Save As.

> Use the Save option to save a file using the same name. If you want to keep the original workbook and save the workbook with the changes under a new name, use Save As.

(continued)

9 At the Save As dialog box, make sure the *Excel S1* folder on your disk is the active folder, key **Excel S1-01** in the File <u>n</u>ame text box, and then press Enter or click <u>S</u>ave at the bottom right corner of the Save As dialog box.

> The Save <u>i</u>n option at the Save As dialog box displays the active folder. If you need to make the *Excel S1* folder on your disk in drive A the active folder, click the down-pointing triangle at the right of the Save <u>i</u>n option and then click 3½ *Floppy (A:)*. Double-click *Excel S1* in the list box. Excel automatically adds the file extension *.xls* to the end of a workbook name.

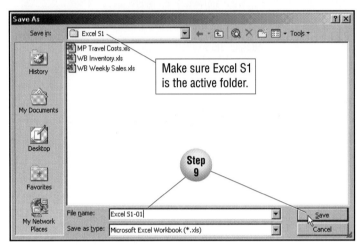

10 Move the cell pointer over the intersection of column H with row 6 and click to make H6 the active cell.

11 Key **1750** and then press Enter.

> Notice that the entry in H7 has changed. This is because the formula created in H7 was dependent on H6. As soon as you enter a value in H6, any other dependent cells are automatically updated. Can you identify other cells that changed as a result of the new value in H6?

	G	H	I
	Friday	Saturday	Total
	1,455.00	1,948.00	9,994.00
	554.00	761.00	3,580.00
	3,175.00		8,213.00
	5,184.00	2,709.00	21,787.00
	198.00	235.00	1,510.00
	84.00	122.00	742.00
	394.00		1,511.00
	676.00	357.00	3,763.00

Step 10

PROBLEM ?

> Keying mistake? Press Backspace to delete the characters to the left of the insertion point and then key the correct text.

12 Make H10 the active cell and then key **371**.

13 Make H14 the active cell and then key **837**.

14 Look at the entry in B19. This percentage is used to calculate the estimated gross profit in row 20 (Total Sales times the Gross Profit Factor). You will change the value in B19 to see the effect on the estimated gross profit values.

	G	H	I
	Friday	Saturday	Total
	1,455.00	1,948.00	9,994.00
	554.00	761.00	3,580.00
	3,175.00	1,750.00	9,963.00
	5,184.00	4,459.00	23,537.00
	198.00	235.00	1,510.00
	84.00	122.00	742.00
	394.00	371.00	1,882.00
	676.00	728.00	4,134.00
	487.00	624.00	4,040.00
	278.00	341.00	1,624.00
	1,267.00	837.00	4,628.00
	2,032.00	1,802.00	10,292.00
	7,892.00	6,989.00	37,963.00

Step 11
Step 12
Step 13

15 Make B19 the active cell, key **24%**, and then press Enter.

Notice the new estimated gross profit values in cells B20 through I20.

Step 15

17	TOTAL SALES	9,567.00	1,674.00	2,353.00	4,351.00	5,137.00	7,892.00	6,989.00	37,963.00
18									
19	Gross Profit Factor	24%							
20	Estimated Gross Profit	2,296.08	401.76	564.72	1,044.24	1,232.88	1,894.08	1,677.36	9,111.12

New Estimated Gross Profit Values as a result of changing BI9.

16 Click the Save button 🖫 on the Standard toolbar.

17 Click the Print button 🖨 on the Standard toolbar.

The worksheet will print on two pages. Later in this section you will learn how to change the page orientation to landscape so that a wide worksheet will fit on one page.

18 Click File and then Close.

Excel displays a gray screen in the Worksheet Area when no workbooks are currently open.

19 Click File and then Exit.

In Addition

AutoComplete

The AutoComplete feature in Excel will complete text entries for you as you start to key a new entry in a cell. If the first few letters that you key match another entry in the column, Excel automatically fills in the remaining text. Press Tab or Enter to accept the text Excel suggests, or continue keying the correct text. You can turn off AutoComplete by clicking Tools and then Options. Click the Edit tab in the Options dialog box and then click the Enable AutoComplete for cell values check box to deselect it. Click OK.

In BRIEF

Start Excel
1 Click Start.
2 Point to *Programs*.
3 Click *Microsoft Excel*.

Open a Workbook
1 Click Open button.
2 Navigate to the desired location and folder.
3 Double-click workbook name.

Save a Workbook with a New Name
1 Click File, Save As.
2 Key the new workbook name.
3 Click Save or press Enter.

1.2 Entering Labels and Values; Using the Fill Handle

A *label* is an entry in a cell that helps the reader relate to the values in the corresponding column or row. Labels are generally entered first when creating a new worksheet since they define the layout of the data in the columns and rows. By default, Excel will align labels at the left edge of the column. A *value* is a number, formula, or function that can be used to perform calculations in the worksheet. By default, Excel will align values at the right edge of the column. Take a few moments to plan or sketch out the layout of a new worksheet before entering labels and values. Decide what calculations you will need to perform and how to display the data so that it will be easily understood and interpreted.

PROJECT: You need to create a new payroll worksheet for The Waterfront Bistro. Begin by entering labels and values.

STEPS

1. Start Excel.

2. Key **Payroll** as the title for the new worksheet in A1.

   When you key a new entry in a cell, the entry appears in the Formula bar as well as within the active cell in the worksheet area. To end a cell entry, press Enter, move to another cell in the worksheet, or click the Enter button on the Formula bar.

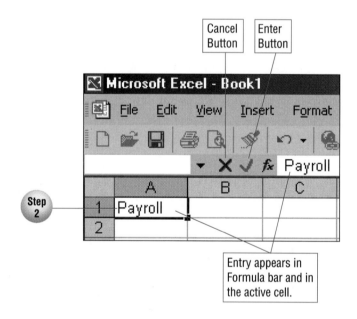

3. Press Enter.

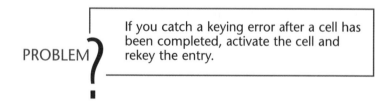

PROBLEM?

If you catch a keying error after a cell has been completed, activate the cell and rekey the entry.

4 Key **Week Ended: September 27, 2003** in A2 and then press Enter.

> Notice the entry in A2 is overflowing into columns B, C, and D. You can allow a label to spill over into adjacent columns as long as you do not plan to enter other data in the overflow cells. In a later section you will see how to adjust column widths.

5 Click the Close button ✕ at the top right corner of the New Workbook Task Pane.

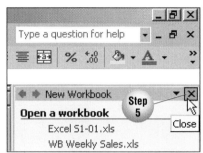

> Closing the task pane will provide a larger viewing area for creating the payroll worksheet. Task panes are context-sensitive and will reappear when a command is being performed that has a task pane associated with it.

6 Enter the remaining labels. (Do not enter the labels for the days of the week except for *Sun*, as this will be done in the following steps.)

	A	B	C	D	E	F	G	H	I	J	K
1	Payroll										
2	Week Ended: September 27, 2003										
3									Total	Pay	Gross
4	Name	Sun							Hours	Rate	Wage
5	Adams										
6	Corvent										
7	Gauthier										
8	Noustadt										
9	Philpott										
10	Su-Lin										
11											
12	Total										
13											

Step 4 · *Step 6*

7 Click B4 to make it the active cell.

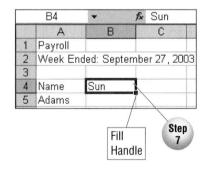

> The active cell is displayed with a thick black border surrounding it. A small black square displays at the bottom right corner of the active cell. This black square is called the *fill handle*. The fill handle is used to fill adjacent cells with the same data or consecutive data. The entries that are automatically inserted in the adjacent cells are dependent on the contents of the active cell. You will use the fill handle in B4 to automatically enter the remaining days of the week in C4 through H4.

8 Point at the fill handle in B4. The cell pointer will change from the large white cross ✛ to a thin black cross ✚ .

(continued)

9 Hold down the left mouse button, drag the pointer to H4, and then release the mouse.

> The entries *Mon* through *Sat* appear in C4 to H4. As you drag the pointer to the right, a gray border surrounds the selected cells and a yellow box will appear below the pointer indicating the label or value that will be inserted. When you release the left mouse button, the cells remain selected and the AutoFill Options button appears. Clicking the AutoFill Options button will cause a drop-down list to appear with various alternatives for how to fill text or data in the cells.

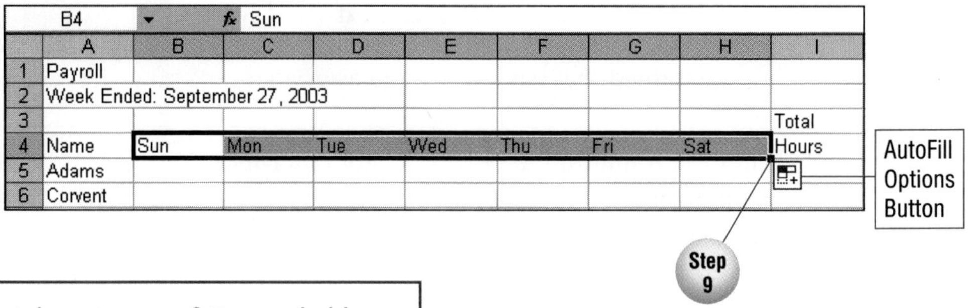

	B4	▾	fx	Sun					
	A	B	C	D	E	F	G	H	I
1	Payroll								
2	Week Ended: September 27, 2003								
3									Total
4	Name	Sun	Mon	Tue	Wed	Thu	Fri	Sat	Hours
5	Adams								
6	Corvent								

AutoFill Options Button

Step 9

PROBLEM **?**

Mon–Sat do not appear? You probably dragged the mouse using the cell pointer instead of the fill handle. This selects cells instead of filling them. Start at step 7 and try again.

10 Click B5 to make it the active cell.

11 Key **8** and then press the right arrow key.

12 Key **5** in C5 and then press the right arrow key.

13 Key the following data in the cells indicated:

D5	=	**6**
E5	=	**8**
F5	=	**7**
G5	=	**0**
H5	=	**6**

14 Make B5 the active cell.

15 Point at the fill handle in B5 and then drag the pointer down to B10.

> This time the active cell contained a value. The value 8 is *copied* to the adjacent cells.

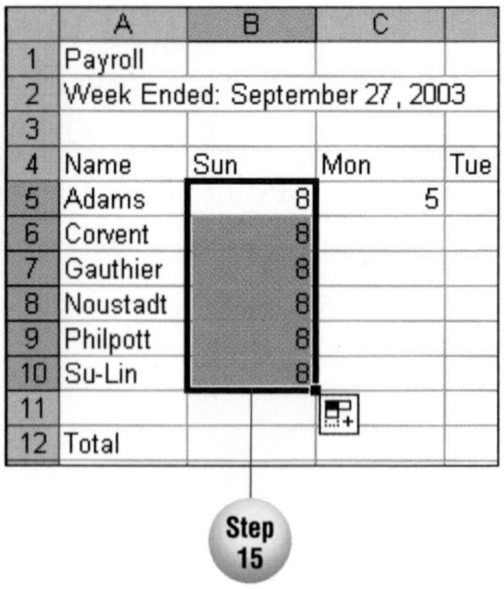

	A	B	C	
1	Payroll			
2	Week Ended: September 27, 2003			
3				
4	Name	Sun	Mon	Tue
5	Adams	8	5	
6	Corvent	8		
7	Gauthier	8		
8	Noustadt	8		
9	Philpott	8		
10	Su-Lin	8		
11				
12	Total			

Step 15

16 Enter the remaining values. Use the fill handle whenever possible to be more efficient.

	A	B	C	D	E	F	G	H	I	J	K
1	Payroll										
2	Week Ended: September 27, 2003										
3									Total	Pay	Gross
4	Name	Sun	Mon	Tue	Wed	Thu	Fri	Sat	Hours	Rate	Wage
5	Adams	8	5	6	8	7	0	6		8.35	
6	Corvent	8	0	7	5	7	5	8		7.75	
7	Gauthier	8	0	0	8	8	8	8	Step	9.15	
8	Noustadt	8	7	5	8	0	0	7	16	7.75	
9	Philpott	8	6	5	5	0	8	8		7.75	
10	Su-Lin	8	0	8	0	8	8	5		7.75	
11											
12	Total										

17 Click the Save button ▣ on the Standard toolbar.

18 At the Save As dialog box, make sure the *Excel S1* folder on your disk is the active folder, key **Excel S1-02** in the File name text box, and then press Enter.

In Addition

More about the Fill Command

Data can also be filled to adjacent cells using the menus. Select the starting cell and the adjacent cells in which you want entries inserted. Click Edit, point to Fill, and then click Down, Right, Up, or Left. The Fill command will correctly enter consecutive data based on the content of the starting cell, e.g., *Monday, Mon, January,* or *Jan.* You can add your own custom lists that will work with the Fill command. To do this, click Tools and then Options. Click the Custom Lists tab in the Options dialog box (shown at the right). Key the list of entries you want the Fill command to insert and then click the Add button. Click OK when finished.

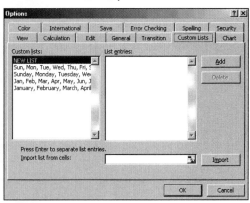

1.3 Performing Calculations Using Formulas

A *formula* is entered into a cell to perform mathematical calculations in a worksheet. All formulas in Excel begin with the equals sign (=) as the first character. After the equals sign, the cell addresses that contain the values you want to calculate are entered between mathematical operators. The mathematical operators are + (addition), - (subtraction), * (multiplication), / (division), and ^ (exponentiation). An example of a valid formula is =A3*B3. The value in A3 is multiplied by the value in B3 and the result is placed in the formula cell. By including the cell address in the formula rather than keying the actual value, you can utilize the powerful recalculation feature in Excel. If you change the contents of a cell that is included in a formula, the worksheet is automatically recalculated so that all values are current.

PROJECT: To calculate total hours and gross pay for the first two employees listed in the payroll worksheet for The Waterfront Bistro, you will use two methods to enter formulas.

STEPS

(1) With Excel S1-02 open, make I5 the active cell.

Begin a formula by activating the cell in which you want the result placed.

(2) Key **=b5+c5+d5+e5+f5+g5+h5** and then press Enter.

The values in B5 through H5 are added and the result, 40, is displayed in I5.

Formula displays in the Formula bar and the cell as it is keyed.

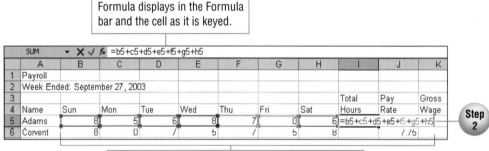

Cell references in the formula are color coded to the originating cell for quick reference and error checking.

Step 2

(3) Press the up arrow key to move the active cell back to I5.

Notice that the result of the formula is displayed in the worksheet area and the formula used to calculate the result is shown in the Formula bar.

(4) Make I6 the active cell, key the formula **=b6+c6+d6+e6+f6+g6+h6**, and then press Enter.

Seem like too much keying? A more efficient way to add a series of cells is available. This method will be introduced after you learn the pointing method for entering formulas.

(5) Make K5 the active cell.

To calculate gross wage you need to multiply the total hours times the pay rate. In steps 6–10, you will enter this formula using the pointing method.

(6) Key the equals sign (=).

(7) Click I5.

A moving dashed border (called a *marquee*) displays around I5, indicating it is the cell you have included in the formula, and a blinking vertical bar (called the *insertion point*) appears in the formula cell K5. Notice also that the Status bar is indicating *Point*.

PROBLEM **?**

> Click the wrong cell by mistake? Simply click the correct cell, or press Esc to start the formula over again.

I	J	K
Total	Pay	Gross
Hours	Rate	Wage
40	8.35	=I5*J5
40	7.75	

Marquee displays around cell J5 in Step 9.

Steps 6–9

8 Key an asterisk (*).

The marquee surrounding cell I5 disappears and I5 is color coded with the cell reference I5 within the formula cell.

9 Click J5.

10 Click the Enter button on the Formula bar or press Enter.

11 Use the pointing method or key the formula **=I6*J6** to calculate the gross wage for Corvent in K6.

12 Click the Save button 💾 on the Standard toolbar.

I	J	K
Total	Pay	Gross
Hours	Rate	Wage
40	8.35	334
40	7.75	310

Step 11

In Addition

Order of Operations

If you include several operators in a formula, Excel calculates the result using the order of operations as follows: negations (i.e., -1) first, then percents (%), then exponentiations (^), then multiplication and division (* and /), and finally addition and subtraction (+ and -). If a formula contains more than one operator at the same level of precedence—for example, both an addition and subtraction operation—Excel calculates the equation from left to right. To change the order of operations, use parentheses around the part of the formula you want calculated first.

Examples:

=B5*C5/D5   Both operators are at the same level of precedence—Excel would multiply the value in B5 times the value in C5 and then divide the result by the value in D5

=(B5+B6+B7)*A10   Excel would add the values in B5 through B7 before multiplying times the value in A10

IN BRIEF

Enter a Formula
1 Activate the formula cell.
2 Key =.
3 Key first cell address.
4 Key operator.
5 Key second cell address.
6 Continue steps 3–5 until finished.
7 Press Enter or click the Enter button.

Enter a Formula Using the Pointing Method
1 Activate the formula cell.
2 Key =.
3 Click the first cell.
4 Key operator.
5 Click the second cell.
6 Repeat steps 3–5 until finished.
7 Press Enter or click the Enter button.

EXCEL

1.4 Using AutoSum

The formulas to calculate the hours worked by the first two employees were rather lengthy. A more efficient way to calculate the total hours for Adams in I5 would be to key the formula =**SUM(B5:I5)**. This formula includes one of Excel's built-in *functions* called SUM. A function is a preprogrammed formula. The structure of a formula utilizing a function begins with the equals sign (=), followed by the name of the function, and then the *argument*. The argument is the term given to the values identified within parentheses. In the example provided, the argument B5:I5 contains the starting cell and the ending cell separated by a colon (:). This is called a *range* and is used when the cells to be added are located in a rectangular-shaped block of cells. Since the SUM function is used frequently, a button named *AutoSum* that will enter the SUM function is available on the Standard toolbar.

PROJECT: The management of The Waterfront Bistro wants you to find a more efficient method of payroll calculation, so you will use AutoSum to complete the hours worked for the payroll worksheet.

STEPS

1 With Excel S1-02 open, make I5 the active cell and then press Delete.

> This deletes the formula in the cell. There was nothing wrong with the formula already entered in I5. You are deleting it so that the formulas in the completed worksheet will be consistent.

2 Click the AutoSum button Σ on the toolbar.

> A moving marquee surrounds cells B5 through H5 and a tooltip appears below the selected range indicating the correct format for the SUM function. Excel enters the formula *=SUM(B5:H5)* in I5. The suggested range B5:H5 is selected within the formula so that you can highlight a different range with the mouse if the suggested range is not correct.

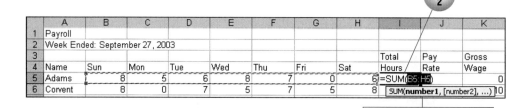

Step 2

Tooltip displays correct format for SUM function.

3 Press Enter.

> Since the range Excel suggests is the correct range, you can finish the formula by pressing Enter, clicking the AutoSum button again, or clicking the Enter button on the Formula bar.

4 With I6 the active cell, press Delete to delete the existing formula in the cell.

5 Click the AutoSum button. When Excel displays the formula *=SUM(B6:H6)*, click the AutoSum button again.

6 Make I7 the active cell and then click the AutoSum button.

> Notice this time the range of cells Excel is suggesting to add (I5:I6) is the wrong range. When you click the AutoSum button, Excel looks for multiple values in the cells immediately above the active cell. If no more than one value exists above the active cell, Excel looks in the cells to the left. In this case there were multiple values above I7. You need to highlight the correct range of cells that you want to add.

7 Position the cell pointer over B7, hold down the left mouse button and drag the pointer to the right to H7, and then release the mouse button.

B	C	D	E	F	G	H	I	J	K
ed: September 27, 2003					**Step 7**				
							Total Hours	Pay Rate	Gross Wage
Sun	Mon	Tue	Wed	Thu	Fri	Sat			
8	5	6	8	7	0	6	40	8.35	334
8	0	7	5	7	5	8	40	7.75	310
8	0	0	8	8	8	8	=SUM(B7:H7)		
							SUM(**number1**, [number2], ...)		
8	7	5	8	0	0	7			
8	6	5	5	0	8	8		7.75	

8 Press Enter.

Now that you have seen how AutoSum operates, you already know that the suggested range for the next employee's total hours will be incorrect. In step 9 you will select the range of cells *first* to avoid the incorrect suggestion.

9 Position the cell pointer over B8, hold down the left mouse button and drag the pointer to the right to I8, and then release the mouse button.

Notice you are including I8, the cell that will display the result, in the range of cells.

10 Click the AutoSum button.

The result, *35*, appears in cell I8.

	A	B	C	D	E	F	G	H	I	
1	Payroll									
2	Week Ended: September 27, 2003									
3									Total	
4	Name	Sun	Mon	Tue	Wed	Thu	Fri	Sat	Hours	
5	Adams	8	5	6	8	7	0	6	40	**Steps 9–10**
6	Corvent	8	0	7	5	7	5	8	40	
7	Gauthier	8	0	0	8	8	8	8	40	
8	Noustadt	8	7	5	8	0	0	7	35	
9	Philpott	8	6	5	5	0	8	8		

11 Click I8 and look in the Formula bar at the formula AutoSum created: *=SUM(B8:H8)*.

If Excel correctly enters the SUM formula from a range of selected cells, it should make sense that you can calculate total hours for more than one employee at the same time using the method employed in steps 9 and 10.

12 Position the cell pointer over B9, hold down the left mouse button, drag the pointer down and to the right to I10, and then release the mouse button.

B	C	D	E	F	G	H	I
ed: September 27, 2003							
							Total
Sun	Mon	Tue	Wed	Thu	Fri	Sat	Hours
8	5	6	8	7	0	6	40
8	0	7	5	7	5	8	40
8	0	0	8	8	8	8	40
8	7	5	8	0	0	7	35
8	6	5	5	0	8	8	40
8	0	8	0	8	8	5	/37

Steps 12–13

13 Click the AutoSum button.

14 Click cells I9 and I10 to confirm that the correct formulas appear in the Formula bar.

15 Click the Save button on the Standard toolbar.

1.5 Copying Relative Formulas

Many times you may create a worksheet in which several formulas are basically the same. For example, in the payroll worksheet, the formula to total the hours for Adams is =SUM(B5:H5), for Corvent =SUM(B6:H6), and so on. The only difference is the row number. Whenever formulas are this similar, you can use the Copy and Paste feature in Excel to copy the formula from one cell to another. The cell containing the original formula is called the *source*, and the cell(s) to which the formula is copied is called the *destination*. When the formula is pasted, Excel automatically changes column letters or row numbers to reflect the destination location. This is referred to as *relative* addressing—the formula is changed relative to its destination.

PROJECT: To simplify your completion of the payroll worksheet for The Waterfront Bistro, you will copy formulas using two methods: Copy and Paste and the fill handle.

STEPS

1 With Excel S1-02 open, make K6 the active cell.

This cell contains the formula =*I6*J6* to calculate the gross wage for Corvent. You will copy this formula to the remaining cells in column K to finish the *Gross Wage* column.

2 Click Edit on the Menu bar and then click Copy.

A moving marquee surrounds the active cell indicating the source. What is being copied is the formula =*I6*J6*—not the value *310*. The contents of the source location are copied to the Clipboard, which is a temporary storage setting.

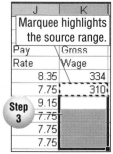

3 Select the range K7:K10. To do this, position the cell pointer over K7, hold down the left mouse button, drag the pointer down to K10, and then release the mouse button.

4 Click Edit on the Menu bar and then click Paste.

Excel copies the formula to the selected cells, displays the results, and the Paste Options button appears. Clicking the Paste Options button will display a drop-down list with various alternatives for pasting the data. The moving marquee remains around the source cell, and the destination cells remain highlighted. The moving marquee will disappear as soon as you start another activity. Press Esc to remove the marquee and the Paste Options button immediately.

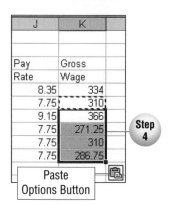

5 Make K7 the active cell and then look at the formula in the Formula bar: =*I7*J7*.

The row number in the source formula was incremented by one to reflect the destination.

6 Use the down arrow key to check the formulas in K8, K9, and K10.

7 Make B12 the active cell.

8 Double-click the AutoSum button.

Double-clicking the AutoSum button inserts the formula *=SUM(B5:B11)* into B12. Since you know that AutoSum looks for multiple values above the active cell for the suggested range, double-clicking is the fastest way to enter this formula. You will now copy the formula using the fill handle.

9 Drag the fill handle to the right to K12.

When the active cell contains a formula, dragging the fill handle causes Excel to copy the formula and change cell references relative to the adjacent cells.

	A	B	C	D	E	F	G	H	I	J	K
1	Payroll										
2	Week Ended: September 27, 2003										
3									Total	Pay	Gross
4	Name	Sun	Mon	Tue	Wed	Thu	Fri	Sat	Hours	Rate	Wage
5	Adams	8	5	6	8	7	0	6	40	8.35	334
6	Corvent	8	0	7	5	7	5	8	40	7.75	310
7	Gauthier	8	0	0	8	8	8	8	40	9.15	366
8	Noustadt	8	7	5	8	0	0	7	35	7.75	271.25
9	Philpott	8	6	5	5	0	8	8	40	7.75	310
10	Su-Lin	8	0	8	0	8	8	5	37	7.75	286.75
11											
12	Total	48	18	31	34	30	29	42	232	48.5	1878

Step 9

PROBLEM? If the results do not appear in C12 through K12, you probably dragged the cell pointer instead of the fill handle. Click B12 and try again.

10 Make J12 the active cell and then press Delete.

The sum of the *Pay Rate* column is not useful information.

11 Make C12 the active cell and look at the formula in the Formula bar: *=SUM(C5:C11).*

The column letter in the source formula was increased by one letter to reflect the destination.

12 Use the right arrow key to check the formulas in the remaining columns.

13 Click the Save button on the Standard toolbar.

In Addition

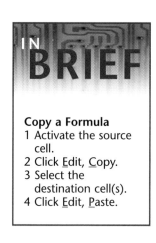

Copy and Paste versus Fill

What is the difference between Copy and Paste and the fill handle? When you use Copy, the contents of the source cell(s) are placed in the Clipboard. The data will remain in the Clipboard and can be pasted several times in the current worksheet or into any other worksheet that is open. Use Copy and Paste when the formula is to be inserted in more than one worksheet or into nonadjacent cells within the current worksheet. Using the fill handle is fast and should be used when the formula is being copied to adjacent cells.

IN BRIEF

Copy a Formula
1 Activate the source cell.
2 Click Edit, Copy.
3 Select the destination cell(s).
4 Click Edit, Paste.

1.6 Testing the Worksheet; Improving the Appearance of Cells

When you have finished building the worksheet, it is a good idea to verify that the formulas you entered are accurate. The worksheet could contain formulas that are correct in structure but not mathematically correct for the situation. For example, the wrong range may be included in a SUM formula, or parentheses missing from a multi-operator formula may cause an incorrect result. Various methods can be employed to verify a worksheet's accuracy. One method is to create a proof formula in a cell beside or below the worksheet that will verify the totals. For example, in the payroll worksheet the *Total Hours* column can be verified by creating a formula that adds all of the hours for all of the employees.

PROJECT: To confirm the accuracy of your calculations in the payroll worksheet for The Waterfront Bistro, you will enter proof formulas to test the worksheet and then use two options for formatting the cells that will improve the worksheet's appearance.

STEPS

1 With Excel S1-02 open, make A14 the active cell.

2 Key **Hours**, press Alt + Enter, key **Proof**, and then press Enter.

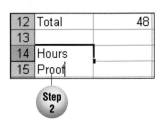

Step 2

> Alt + Enter is the command to insert a hard return in a cell. This command is used when you want multiple lines within the same cell. The height of the row is automatically expanded to accommodate the multiple lines.

3 Make B14 the active cell.

4 Click in the Formula bar, key **=sum(b5:h10),** and then click the Enter button or press Enter. (Alternatively, you could click the AutoSum button and then drag the pointer across the range B5 through H10.)

> Excel displays the result, *232*, which verifies that your total hours are correct. Can you think of another formula that would have accomplished the same objective? *(Hint: Think of the direction you added to arrive at the total hours in I12.)*

PROBLEM **?**

> Didn't get 232? Then one of the cell entries is incorrect. Look through previous pages to see if the difference between 232 and your result equals a cell entry that you missed.

Step 4

Keyed range is color coded with worksheet range for a quick reference and error checking.

	A	B	C	D	E	F	G	H
	SUM	▾ ✕ ✓ ƒx =sum(b5:h10)						
1	Payroll							
2	Week Ended: September 27, 2003							
3								
4	Name	Sun	Mon	Tue	Wed	Thu	Fri	Sat
5	Adams	8	5	6	8	7	0	6
6	Corvent	8	0	7	5	7	5	8
7	Gauthier	8	0	0	8	8	8	8
8	Noustadt	8	7	5	8	0	0	7
9	Philpott	8	6	5	5	0	8	8
10	Su-Lin	8	0	8	0	8	8	5
11								
12	Total	48	18	31	34	30	29	42
13								
14	Hours Proof	'b5:h10)						

5 Make A15 the active cell.

6 Key **Gross**, press Alt + Enter, key **Wage**, press Alt + Enter, key **Proof**, and then press Enter.

7 Make B15 the active cell.

Checking the *Gross Wage* column is not as straightforward as checking the *Total Hours*. For this example, you will calculate the first gross wage using the values instead of the cell addresses. Using the assumption that the formula was copied, it is safe to suppose that the remaining gross wage amounts are correct. As a final check, you will sum the *Gross Wage* column again. *(Note: In a small worksheet such as this one, it is feasible to quickly review each gross wage formula to ensure that the correct cells are being multiplied. The method described in steps 6–9 is useful for larger worksheets.)*

8 Key **=40*8.35** and then press the right arrow key.

12	Total	48
13		
	Hours	
14	Proof	232
	Gross	
	Wage	
15	Proof	=40*8.35

The result, 334, confirms that the formula in K5 is correct. (Notice that in step 8 Excel was used to calculate a value in a cell similar to how one might use an electronic calculator.)

Step 8

9 With C15 the active cell, key **=sum(k5:k10)** and then press Enter.

The result, 1878, confirms that the total for the *Gross Wage* column is correct. The importance of testing a worksheet cannot be emphasized enough. Worksheets often contain financial or statistical data that is crucial for an organization. These worksheets can form the basis for strategic decisions by management. A worksheet containing incorrect formulas can lead to disastrous consequences.

	A	B	C	D	E	F	G	H	I	J	K
1	Payroll										
2	Week Ended: September 27, 2003										
3									Total	Pay	Gross
4	Name	Sun	Mon	Tue	Wed	Thu	Fri	Sat	Hours	Rate	Wage
5	Adams	8	5	6	8	7	0	6	40	8.35	334
6	Corvent	8	0	7	5	7	5	8	40	7.75	310
7	Gauthier	8	0	0	8	8	8	8	40	9.15	366
8	Noustadt	8	7	5	8	0	0	7	35	7.75	271.25
9	Philpott	8	6	5	5	0	8	8	40	7.75	310
10	Su-Lin	8	0	8	0	8	8	5	37	7.75	286.75
11											
12	Total	48	18	31	34	30	29	42	232		1878
13											
	Hours										
14	Proof	232									
	Gross										
	Wage										
15	Proof	334	1878								

Formulas tested correctly.

Step 9

10 Select the range K5:K12.

These final steps in building a worksheet are meant to improve the appearance of cells. In the range K5 through K12 notice that some of the values show no decimals while others show 2 decimal places. Excel uses up to 15 decimal places for precision when calculating values. Since the *Gross Wage* column is representing a sum of money that would be paid to employees, you will format these cells to the Currency format.

(continued)

⑪ Click Format and then Cells.

⑫ In the Format Cells dialog box with the Number tab selected, click *Currency* in the Category list box and then click OK.

> The Currency format adds a dollar sign, a comma in thousands, and two decimal places to each value in the selection.

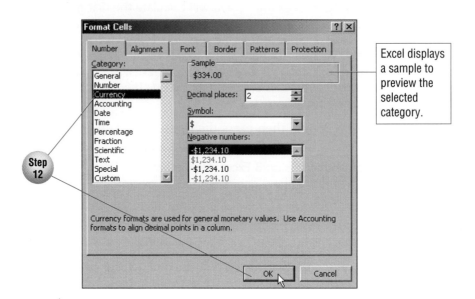

⑬ Select the range B15:C15, and then apply the Currency format. (If necessary, refer to steps 10–12 for assistance.)

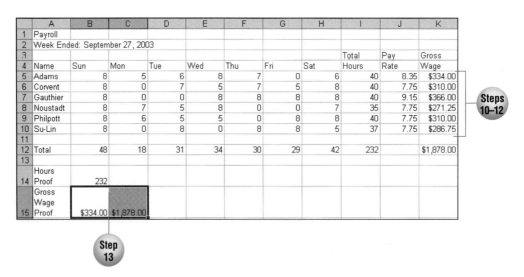

⑭ Select the range B3:K4.

> As previously mentioned, labels are aligned at the left edge of a column while values are aligned at the right edge. In the next step you will align the labels at the right edge of the column so they appear directly over the values they represent.

⑮ Click Format and then Cells.

16 Click the Alignment tab in the Format Cells dialog box.

17 Click the down-pointing triangle to the right of the Horizontal text box (currently displays *General*) and then click *Right (Indent)*.

18 Click OK.

19 Click in any cell outside the highlighted range to deselect the cells.

> Additional formatting options that can be used to enhance a worksheet's appearance will be covered in a later section.

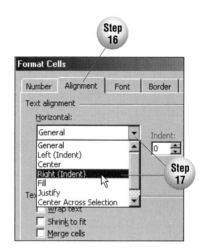

Step 16

Step 17

Steps 14–19

	A	B	C	D	E	F	G	H	I	J	K
1	Payroll										
2	Week Ended: September 27, 2003										
3									Total	Pay	Gross
4	Name	Sun	Mon	Tue	Wed	Thu	Fri	Sat	Hours	Rate	Wage
5	Adams	8	5	6	8	7	0	6	40	8.35	$334.00
6	Corvent	8	0	7	5	7	5	8	40	7.75	$310.00
7	Gauthier	8	0	0	8	8	8	8	40	9.15	$366.00
8	Noustadt	8	7	5	8	0	0	7	35	7.75	$271.25
9	Philpott	8	6	5	5	0	8	8	40	7.75	$310.00
10	Su-Lin	8	0	8	0	8	8	5	37	7.75	$286.75
11											
12	Total	48	18	31	34	30	29	42	232		$1,878.00
13											
14	Hours Proof	232									
15	Gross Wage Proof	$334.00	$1,878.00								

20 Click the Save button on the Standard toolbar.

In Addition

Setting the Standard and Formatting Toolbars to Occupy Two Rows

When you install Office XP, the default setting is for the Standard and Formatting toolbars to share the same row. This means that several buttons from each toolbar are not visible. You can instruct Excel to use two rows to display the Standard and Formatting toolbars, thereby allowing you to see all of the available buttons on each toolbar. Click Tools, Customize, and then select the Options tab in the Customize dialog box, as shown at the right. Click the Show Standard and Formatting toolbars on two rows check box to select the option, and then click Close.

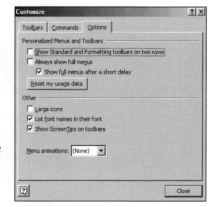

1.7 Using Help

An extensive online help resource is available whenever you are working in Excel by clicking the text inside the Ask a Question box located at the right side of the Menu bar, keying a term, phrase, or question, and then pressing Enter. This invokes the online help facility from which you can locate information by clicking any of the topics displayed in the results list. If the topic you need assistance with is not displayed, try keying another term or click the None of the above, search for more on the Web option at the bottom of the list. This will connect you with the Microsoft Office Web site where you can search for more information.

PROJECT: After reviewing the payroll worksheet, the manager of The Waterfront Bistro thinks the first two title rows would look better if they were centered over the columns in the worksheet. You will use the Ask a Question feature to find out how to do this.

S T E P S

① With Excel S1-02 open, make A1 the active cell.

② Click the text inside the Ask a Question text box (currently reads *Type a question for help*) at the right end of the Menu bar.

> When you click the Ask a Question box, an insertion point will appear and the text *Type a question for help* disappears. Once you have completed an initial search for help using the Ask a Question box, the down-pointing triangle to the right of the text box will display a list of topics previously searched for in help.

③ Key **Center over columns** and then press Enter.

> A list of help topics related to the term, phrase, or question appears below the Ask a Question box.

④ Click *Merge or split cells or data*.

> As you move the mouse pointer over a help topic, the pointer changes to a hand with the index finger pointing upward. When you click a topic, the help information displays in a separate Microsoft Excel Help window. You can continue clicking topics and reading the information in the Help window until you have found what you are looking for.

⑤ Click *Spread the content of one cell over many cells*.

> The Help window expands below the selected topic to display information on the feature including the steps to complete the task. Blue underlined text, called a *hyperlink*, means that further information can be displayed when the link is clicked.

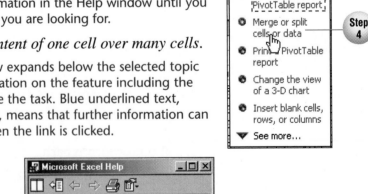

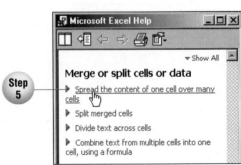

EXCEL

22

SECTION 1: ANALYZING DATA USING EXCEL

6 Read the information in the Spread the content of one cell over many cells section.

7 Click the Close button **✕** on the Microsoft Excel Help window Title bar.

8 Select the range A1:K1.

9 Click the Merge and Center button ▦ on the Formatting toolbar.

A1 is merged across columns A through K and the text *Payroll* is automatically centered within the merged cell.

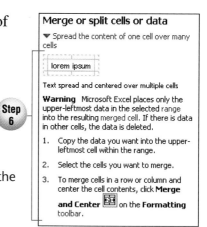

Merge or split cells or data

▼ Spread the content of one cell over many cells

| lorem ipsum |

Text spread and centered over multiple cells

Warning Microsoft Excel places only the upper-leftmost data in the selected range into the resulting merged cell. If there is data in other cells, the data is deleted.

1. Copy the data you want into the upper-leftmost cell within the range.

2. Select the cells you want to merge.

3. To merge cells in a row or column and center the cell contents, click **Merge and Center** ▦ on the **Formatting** toolbar.

Step 6

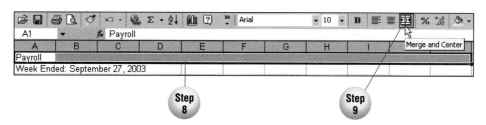

Step 8

Step 9

10 Select the range A2:K2 and then click the Merge and Center button.

The two titles in the payroll worksheet are now centered over the cells below them.

11 Click the Save button on the Standard toolbar.

Step 10

	A	B	C	D	E	F	G	H	I	J	K
1						Payroll					
2					Week Ended: September 27, 2003						
3									Total	Pay	Gross
4	Name	Sun	Mon	Tue	Wed	Thu	Fri	Sat	Hours	Rate	Wage
5	Adams	8	5	6	8	7	0	6	40	8.35	$334.00
6	Corvent	8	0	7	5	7	5	8	40	7.75	$310.00
7	Gauthier	8	0	0	8	8	8	8	40	9.15	$366.00
8	Noustadt	8	7	5	8	0	0	7	35	7.75	$271.25
9	Philpott	8	6	5	5	0	8	8	40	7.75	$310.00
10	Su-Lin	8	0	8	0	8	8	5	37	7.75	$286.75
11											
12	Total	48	18	31	34	30	29	42	232		$1,878.00
13											
14	Hours Proof	232									
15	Gross Wage Proof	$334.00	$1,878.00								

In Addition

The Office Assistant

Office XP includes an animated Office Assistant that can be displayed while you are working. To turn on the Office Assistant, click Help and then Show the Office Assistant. The Office Assistant will provide information about specific topics, and sometimes will provide tips while you are working based on the actions you have just performed. Tips are indicated when the yellow lightbulb appears over the animated assistant. Click the lightbulb to read the tip and then click OK. To access online help from the assistant, click the Office Assistant, key a question, and then click Search.

In Brief

Use Help
1 Click text inside Ask a Question box.
2 Key a term, phrase, or question.
3 Press Enter.
4 Click a topic from the results list.
5 If necessary, continue selecting topics or hyperlinks.
6 Close the Microsoft Help window.

1.8 Previewing, Printing, and Closing a Workbook

Most of the time you will print a worksheet to have a paper copy, or *hard copy*, to file or to attach to a memo, letter, or report. Large, complex worksheets are often easier to proofread and check from a paper copy. The Print button on the Standard toolbar will print the active worksheet in the open workbook. If more than one worksheet exists in a workbook, open the Print dialog box by clicking File and Print, and then change the Print what option to Entire workbook. Use the Print Preview feature before printing to view how the page will appear when printed. This allows you to check whether the entire worksheet will fit on one page, and to view other page layout options.

PROJECT: The payroll worksheet for The Waterfront Bistro is finished, so you want to preview its appearance and then print it.

STEPS

1 With Excel S1-02 open, make A17 the active cell, key **Worksheet prepared by: Student Name** (substitute your first and last name for *Student Name*), and then press Enter.

> Check with your instructor before proceeding to see if you should add other identifying information such as student number and class number.

2 Click the Print Preview button 🔍 on the Standard toolbar to display the worksheet in the Print Preview window shown in Figure E1.2.

FIGURE E1.2 Print Preview Window

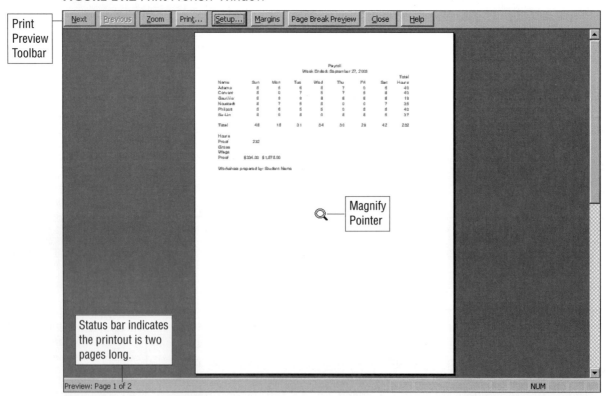

Print Preview Toolbar

Magnify Pointer

Status bar indicates the printout is two pages long.

Preview: Page 1 of 2   NUM

3 The Print Preview window displays a picture of what the printed page will look like. Notice the Status bar is indicating *Page 1 of 2*. Click the Next button on the Print Preview toolbar.

④ The second page of the printout appears showing the columns that could not fit on page 1. The mouse pointer displays as a magnifying glass 🔍 in the Print Preview screen. Move the mouse pointer over the two columns and click the left mouse button.

> This causes the display to enlarge so that you can read the data in the columns.

⑤ Click the mouse to return to the full-page view and then click the Previous button on the Print Preview toolbar.

⑥ Click the Setup button on the Print Preview toolbar.

> One of the methods that can be used to reduce the printout to one page is to change the orientation of the paper from portrait to landscape. In *portrait* orientation, the page is printed on paper taller than it is wide. In *landscape* orientation, the data is rotated to print on paper that is wider than it is tall.

⑦ If necessary, click the Page tab in the Page Setup dialog box, click Landscape in the Orientation section, and then click OK.

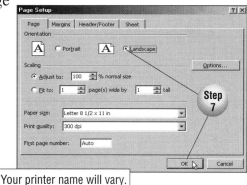

> The Print Preview screen will change to show how the worksheet will appear in landscape orientation. Notice that all of the columns now fit on one page.

⑧ Click the Print button on the Print Preview toolbar.

> The Print Preview screen closes and the Print dialog box appears.

Your printer name will vary.

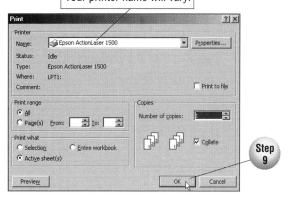

⑨ The default settings in the Print dialog box are to print one copy of All pages in the Active sheet(s). Make any necessary changes to the settings in the Print dialog box and then click OK.

> In a few seconds the worksheet will print.

⑩ Click the right scroll arrow ▶ a few times until you can see columns M and N.

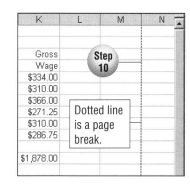

Step 10

Dotted line is a page break.

> The dotted vertical line between columns M and N is a page break. Page breaks appear after you have used Print Preview or Print and indicate how much information can fit on a page.

⑪ Click the Save button on the Standard toolbar.

⑫ Click File and then Close.

> Excel displays a gray screen in the worksheet area when no workbooks are currently open.

1.9 Navigating a Worksheet

So far, you have been working with small worksheets that generally fit within the viewing area in the screen. Once worksheets become larger you will need to scroll to the right or scroll down to locate cells with which you need to work. The horizontal and vertical scroll bars are used to scroll with the mouse. Scrolling using the scroll bars does not move the position of the active cell. You can also scroll using the arrow keys or with keyboard commands. Scrolling using the keyboard moves the active cell.

PROJECT: To prepare for the creation of another report, you will open a workbook and practice various scrolling techniques using the mouse and the keyboard.

STEPS

① Click the Open button [icon] on the Standard toolbar.

② At the Open dialog box with *Excel S1* the active folder, double-click the workbook *WB Inventory*.

③ Position the mouse pointer on the down-pointing triangle at the bottom of the vertical scroll bar and then click the left mouse button five times to scroll down the worksheet.

④ Position the mouse pointer on the right-pointing triangle at the right edge of the horizontal scroll bar and then click the left mouse button five times to scroll to the right edge of the worksheet.

⑤ Position the mouse pointer on the scroll box in the horizontal scroll bar, hold down the left mouse button, drag the scroll box to the left edge of the horizontal scroll bar, and then release the mouse button.

> The width or height of the scroll box indicates the proportional amount of the used cells in the worksheet that are visible in the current window. The position of the scroll box indicates the relative location of the visible cells within the remainder of the worksheet.

Step 3

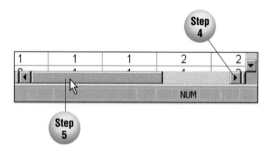

Step 4

Step 5

⑥ Position the mouse pointer on the scroll box in the vertical scroll bar, hold down the left mouse button, drag the scroll box to the top of the vertical scroll bar, and then release the mouse button.

> You are now back to viewing the beginning of the worksheet.

⑦ Click Edit and then Go To.

8 At the Go To dialog box, key **O54** in the <u>R</u>eference text box and then click OK or press Enter.

> The active cell is positioned in O54, which is the total of all of the inventory units.

PROBLEM ?

If you receive the message *Reference is not valid* after you press Enter, you have probably keyed zero instead of the letter *O*. Click OK at the message box and try again.

9 Press Ctrl + Home.

> Ctrl + Home moves the active cell to A1.

10 Press Page Down twice.

> Each time you press Page Down you move down one screen.

11 Press the right arrow key four times.

> Each time you press the right arrow key, you move the active cell one cell to the right.

12 Use the up, down, left, and right arrow keys to practice moving around the worksheet.

> Holding down a directional arrow key will cause the screen to scroll very quickly. Table E1.2 illustrates more keyboard scrolling techniques.

13 Close WB Inventory and then Exit Excel.

TABLE E1.2 Keyboard Movement Commands

Press	To move to
Arrow keys	One cell up, down, left, or right
Ctrl + Home	A1
Ctrl + End	Last cell in worksheet
Home	Beginning of row
Page Down	Down one screen
Page Up	Up one screen
Alt + Page Down	One screen to the right
Alt + Page Up	One screen to the left

In Addition

Smart Tags

A new feature of Microsoft Office XP is the ability of the application to recognize certain types of data and present the user with a menu to perform actions on the data. The options on the Smart Tags Actions menu will depend on the data that has been recognized. For example, if you key in a cell the name of a person to whom you recently sent e-mail from Outlook, a menu will appear with options to Send Mail, Schedule a Meeting, and so on. A Smart Tag is indicated in Excel by a purple triangle at the bottom right corner of the cell. Point to the purple triangle and the Smart Tag Actions button will appear, as shown at the right. By default, smart tags are turned off. To turn them on, display the AutoCorrect Options dialog box with the Smart Tags tab selected and then click the Label data with smart tags check box.

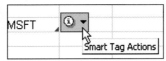

IN BRIEF

Go to a Specific Cell
1 Click <u>E</u>dit and <u>G</u>o To.
2 Key cell address.
3 Click OK.

FEATURES SUMMARY

Feature	Button	Menu	Keyboard
Align Right	☰	F̲ormat, C̲ells, Alignment, Horizontal	
AutoSum	Σ		
Close a workbook	✕	F̲ile, C̲lose	Ctrl + F4
Copy	▤	E̲dit, C̲opy	Ctrl + C
Currency Style Format	$	F̲ormat, C̲ells, Number	
Exit Excel	✕	F̲ile, E̲xit	Alt + F4
Fill Down		E̲dit, F̲ill, D̲own	Ctrl + D
Fill Right		E̲dit, F̲ill, R̲ight	Ctrl + R
Fill Up		E̲dit, F̲ill, U̲p	
Fill Left		E̲dit, F̲ill, L̲eft	
Go To		E̲dit, G̲o To	Ctrl + G
Help	Type a question for help	Help, Microsoft Excel H̲elp	F1
Merge and Center	▦	F̲ormat, C̲ells, Alignment, M̲erge cells	
Open	▱	F̲ile, O̲pen	Ctrl + O
Paste	▤	E̲dit, P̲aste	Ctrl + V
Print	▤	F̲ile, P̲rint	Ctrl + P
Print Preview	▣	F̲ile, Print Previ̲ew	
Save	▤	F̲ile, S̲ave	Ctrl + S
Save As		F̲ile, Save A̲s	F12

PROCEDURES CHECK

Look at the Excel screen in Figure E1.3. This screen contains numbers with lines pointing to specific items. Identify after the number below the item that corresponds with the number in the Excel screen.

1. _____

2. _____

3. _____

4. _____

5. _____

6. _____

7. _____

8. _____

FIGURE E1.3

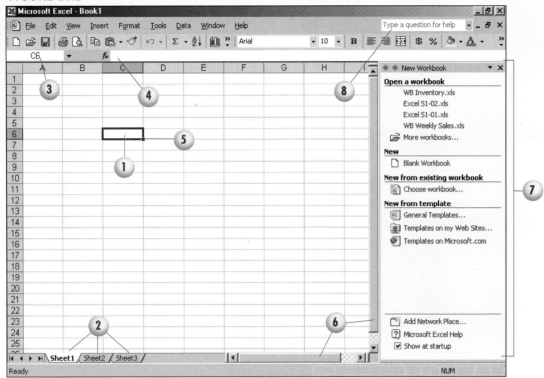

Matching: Identify the following buttons:

9. _____

10. _____

11. _____

12. _____

13. _____

14. _____

15. _____

SKILLS REVIEW

Activity 1: ENTERING LABELS AND VALUES; FORMATTING CELLS

1. Start Excel and then close the New Workbook Task Pane.

2. Create the workbook shown in Figure E1.4. Use the fill handle whenever possible to facilitate data entry. In rows 8, 13, and 17 press the spacebar twice before keying to indent the text.

3. Select the range D6:G17 and then complete the following steps:

    a. Display the Format Cells dialog box.

    b. Choose *Currency* in the *C*ategory list box.

FIGURE E1.4 Activity 1

	A	B	C	D	E	F	G
1	The Waterfront Bistro						
2	Condensed Quarterly Statement of Income						
3	For the Quarter Ended September 30, 2003						
4	In Thousands						
5				Jul	Aug	Sep	Total
6	Sales			50	38	37	
7	Cost of Goods Sold			34	21	19	
8	Gross Margin						
9							
10	Advertising Expense			1	1	1	
11	Office Expense			5	5	5	
12	Miscellaneous Expense			1	1	1	
13	Total Expenses						
14							
15	Net Income Before Taxes						
16	Taxes						
17	Net Income After Taxes						

  c Click OK.

  d Deselect the range.

 4 Save the workbook and name it Excel S1-R1.

Activity 2: ENTERING FORMULAS; USING AUTOSUM

 1 With Excel S1-R1 open, create the following formulas by keying them in the Formula bar or the cell, using the pointing method, or by clicking the AutoSum button:

  a In cell D8, subtract Cost of Goods Sold from Sales by entering *=D6-D7*.

  b In cell D13, add the three expenses by entering *=SUM(D10:D12)*.

  c In cell D15, subtract Total Expenses from Gross Margin by entering *=D8-D13*.

  d In cell D16, multiply Net Income Before Taxes by 22% by entering *=D15*22%*.

  e In cell D17, subtract Taxes from Net Income Before Taxes by entering *=D15-D16*.

 2 Copy and paste formulas in column D to columns E and F as follows:

  a Select D8 and then copy and paste the formula to the range E8:F8.

  b Select D13 and then copy and paste the formula to the range E13:F13. *(Hint: The Clipboard Task Pane will appear when you copy a second item. This task pane will be covered in a later section. For now, close the task pane. If a message displays saying the Clipboard Task Pane will not display again, click OK.)*

  c Select D15:D17 and then copy and paste the formulas to the range E15:F17.

 3 Click in cell G6 and then click the AutoSum button to enter the formulas to add D6:F6. Using the AutoSum button, enter in the remaining cells in column G the formulas required to total columns D, E, and F.

 4 Save Excel S1-R1.

Activity 3: IMPROVING THE APPEARANCE OF THE WORKSHEET; PREVIEWING AND PRINTING

 1 With Excel S1-R1 open, select the range A1:G1 and then click the Merge and Center button.

 2 Merge and center A2, A3, and A4 by completing steps similar to that in step 1.

 3 Select the range D5:G5, display the Format Cells dialog box, click the Alignment tab, and then change the horizontal alignment to *Right (Indent)*. Click OK.

 4 Deselect the range and then click the Print Preview button.

 5 Close the Print Preview screen and then click the Print button.

 6 Save Excel S1-R1.

Activity 4: USING ASK A QUESTION BOX

 1 With Excel S1-R1 open, click the text inside the Ask a Question box, key **decrease decimal places**, and then press Enter.

 2 Click *Change the number of decimal places displayed* in the topic list.

 3 Read the information displayed in Help and then close the Help window.

 4 Select the range D16:G17 and then decrease the number of decimal places to zero.

 5 Deselect D16:G17.

 6 Save, print, and then close Excel S1-R1.

PERFORMANCE PLUS

Activity 1: ADDING LABELS, VALUES, AND FORMULAS TO A WORKSHEET

1 Open MP Travel Costs.
2 Save the workbook with Save As and name it Excel S1-P1.
3 You have received a message from Melissa Gehring of First Choice Travel with quotations for return airfare, hotel, and airport transfers for the film crew to travel to Toronto for the location shoot July 7 to August 29, 2003. This information is summarized below.
   - Return Air Fare is $533.20 per person
   - Melissa has negotiated a room rate of $5,700.00 per room for the entire duration with two persons per room
   - Airport Transfer Limousine Service is a flat rate of $550.00 in Toronto and $475.00 in Los Angeles
   - All of the above prices include taxes and are quoted in U.S. dollars
4 Enter the appropriate labels, values, and formulas to complete the worksheet.
5 Make any formatting changes you think would improve the appearance of the worksheet.
6 Save, print, and then close Excel S1-P1.

Activity 2: CREATING A WORKBOOK

1 You are Bobbie Sinclair, business manager at Performance Threads. You are preparing a price estimate for costumes needed by Marquee Productions for its Toronto film shoot July 7 to August 29, 2003. Create a new workbook that will calculate the costume costs using the following information:
   a Click the New button on the Standard toolbar to open a blank worksheet.
   b 5 costumes must be researched, designed, and custom made at $2,500.00 per costume. Marquee Productions will own these costumes after the film shoot.
   c 7 costumes are in stock and can be rented at $110.00 per day. Marquee Productions has advised that it will need these costumes for 16 days.
   d 18 costumes require size and length adjustments. These costumes are subject to the same rental fee, but are only required for 12 days. A flat fee for alterations is $122.50 per costume.
2 Make any formatting changes you think would improve the appearance of the worksheet.
3 Save the workbook and name it Excel S1-P2.
4 Print and then close Excel S1-P2.

Activity 3: CREATING A WORKBOOK

1 You are Sam Vestering, manager of North American Distribution for Worldwide Enterprises. You are preparing a projected distribution revenue schedule for Marquee Productions' latest film *Two By Two*, to be released February 14, 2003. Create a new workbook that will estimate Worldwide's projected revenue using the following information (see Figure E1.5):

a   Preview cities receive the film on the Friday before the general release date and pay Worldwide Enterprises 1.25% of projected box office revenues.

b   General release cities pay Worldwide Enterprises 1% of projected box office revenues.

c   All projections are paid in U.S. dollars.

d   Include a total of the projected revenue for Worldwide Enterprises. *(Hint: You may want to create this workbook by grouping the preview cities and the general release cities separately.*

FIGURE E1.5 Activity 3

City	Release Category	Projected Box Office Sales in Millions
New York	Preview	22.5
Phoenix	General	12.3
Los Angeles	Preview	31.8
Denver	Preview	18.3
Miami	General	22.5
Des Moines	General	11.2
Wichita	Preview	10.6
Boston	General	19.4

City	Release Category	Projected Box Office Sales in Millions
Philadelphia	General	21.6
Fort Worth	General	19.4
Milwaukee	General	17.8
Vancouver	General	12.4
Winnipeg	General	10.1
Toronto	Preview	17.5
Montreal	Preview	15.8

2   Make any formatting changes you think would improve the appearance of the workbook.

3   Save the workbook and name it Excel S1-P3.

4   Print and then close Excel S1-P3.

Activity 4: FINDING INFORMATION ON HIDING ZERO VALUES

1   Using the Ask a Question box, find out how to display or hide zero values on an entire worksheet.

2   Click the Print button on the Microsoft Excel Help window toolbar to print the help topic that you find and then close the Help window.

3   Open WB Inventory.

4   Save the workbook with Save As and name it Excel S1-P4.

5   Hide the zero values.

6   Display the Print dialog box, change the Print range to print page 1 to 1, and then click OK.

7   Save and then close Excel S1-P4.

Activity 5: LOCATING EXCEL HELP FROM OFFICE ON THE WEB

1   Display a new blank worksheet.

2   Click Help and then Office on the Web.

3   If necessary, scroll down the Microsoft Office Assistance Center page to the Help By Product section and then click *Excel*.

4   Scroll down the Excel Help Articles page to the Working With Data section.

5   Click the link *Frequently Asked Questions About Entering Data in Excel 2002*.

6   Click the link *What characters can be used as numbers?* and then read the information displayed below the link.

7   Click the link *How do I enter numbers as text?* and then read the information displayed below the link.

8   Close Internet Explorer and then close the worksheet.

Editing and Formatting Worksheets

Several techniques are available in Excel to change the content of cells or the layout of the worksheet. Formatting features are used to improve the appearance of the data and, when used strategically, can draw the reader's attention to a cell or series of cells deemed important. In this section you will learn the skills and complete the projects described here.

 Note: Before beginning this section, delete the Excel S1 *folder on your disk. Next, copy to your disk the* Excel S2 *subfolder from the* Excel *folder on the CD that accompanies this textbook, and then make* Excel S2 *the active folder.*

Projects

 Edit and format a quotation and invoice for catering services and format an inventory report.

 Edit and format a costume cost schedule and complete an invoice for costume production.

 Edit and format a revenue summary report for movie distribution.

Skills

- Edit the content of cells
- Clear cells and cell formats
- Perform a spell check
- Insert and delete cells, columns, and rows
- Use Undo and Redo
- Hide and unhide columns and rows
- Move and copy cells
- Adjust column width and row height
- Freeze and unfreeze panes
- Change the zoom percentage
- Change the font, size, style, and color of cells
- Apply numeric formats and adjust the number of decimal places
- Change cell alignment and indentation
- Add borders and shading
- Autoformat a worksheet
- Find and replace cell entries and formats

2.1 Editing and Clearing Cells; Performing a Spell Check

The contents of a cell can be edited directly within the cell or in the Formula bar. Clearing a cell can involve removing the cell contents or format, or both. The spell check feature is a useful tool to assist with correcting keying errors within a worksheet. After completing a spell check you will still need to proofread the worksheet, since the spelling checker will not highlight all errors and cannot check the accuracy of values.

PROJECT: Dana Hirsch, manager of The Waterfront Bistro, has asked you to complete a quotation for catering services to be provided to Marquee Productions at its Toronto filming location.

S T E P S

1 Open WB Quotation. *(Note: This worksheet contains intentional spelling errors that will be corrected in steps 11-14.)*

2 Double-click I21.

> Double-clicking a cell inserts a blinking insertion point in the cell indicating the *Edit* mode has been activated; *Edit* appears in the Status bar. The location of the insertion point within the cell will vary depending on where the cell pointer was positioned when *Edit* mode was activated.

3 Press the right or left arrow key as needed to move the insertion point between the decimal point and 8, and then press the Delete key.

4 Key **9** and then press Enter.

5 Make I27 the active cell.

6 Move the pointer after the last 8 in the Formula bar and then click the left mouse button.

> The cell pointer changes to an I-beam pointer when positioned on the Formula bar.

7 Press Backspace to delete the 8, key **3**, and then click the Enter button on the Formula bar.

8 Make A9 the active cell and then press Delete.

> Pressing Delete or Backspace will clear the contents of the active cell. Any formats or comments applied to the cell remain active.

9 Select the range I17:I18, click <u>E</u>dit, point to Cle<u>a</u>r, and then click A<u>l</u>l.

> Use the Clear All feature to remove everything from a cell including formats or comments.

10 Press Ctrl + Home to move the active cell to A1.

11 Click <u>T</u>ools and <u>S</u>pelling.

> A spell check begins at the active cell and compares words within the worksheet with words in the dictionary. Words that do not match are highlighted as potential errors. Buttons in the Spelling dialog box are used to skip the word (<u>I</u>gnore Once or I<u>g</u>nore All), replace the word with the highlighted word in the Suggestio<u>n</u>s list box (<u>C</u>hange), or add the word to the dictionary (<u>A</u>dd to Dictionary) if it is spelled correctly.

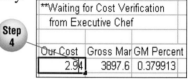

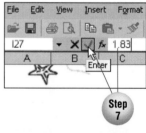

12 Click the Change button in the Spelling dialog box to replace *Torontow* with *Toronto*.

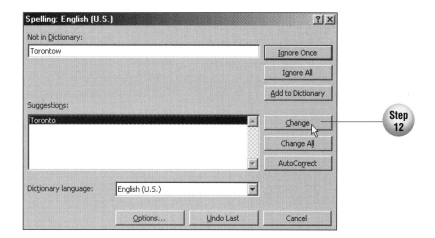

13 Click the Change button in the Spelling dialog box to replace *Persns* with *Persons*.

14 Complete the spell check, changing words as required. Click OK at the message that the spelling check is complete.

> If the correct word is not initially selected in the Suggestions list box, double-click to select the correct spelling. If the correct spelling does not appear in the Suggestions list box, click in the Not in Dictionary text box, insert and/or delete characters as required, and then click Change. Drag the Spelling dialog box out of the way if you need to see the selected word within the worksheet.

15 Save the workbook with Save As and name it Excel S2-01.

In Addition

AutoCorrect

The AutoCorrect feature will automatically correct common typographical errors as you key. For example, if you key *teh* and press the spacebar, Excel will automatically change *teh* to *the*. Click Tools and then AutoCorrect Options to add your own frequently misspelled words to the AutoCorrect list, shown at the right. Key the word the way you misspell it in the Replace text box, key the correct spelling in the With text box, and then click Add.

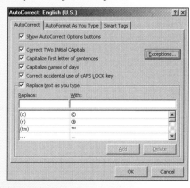

In BRIEF

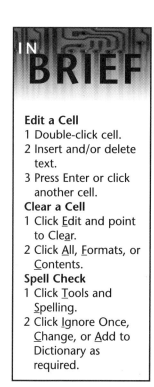

Edit a Cell
1 Double-click cell.
2 Insert and/or delete text.
3 Press Enter or click another cell.

Clear a Cell
1 Click Edit and point to Clear.
2 Click All, Formats, or Contents.

Spell Check
1 Click Tools and Spelling.
2 Click Ignore Once, Change, or Add to Dictionary as required.

2.2 Inserting and Deleting Cells; Using Undo and Redo

Insert cells if you need to add data to the worksheet. Existing cells can be shifted right or down in the worksheet. Previously you learned how to use Delete and Clear to remove the contents from cells. The existing cell was emptied and remained in the worksheet. Using the Delete command from the Edit menu will cause surrounding cells to shift to fill in the gap created by the deleted cells. Undo will reverse the last action or delete the last text keyed. Click the down-pointing triangle next to the Undo button on the Standard toolbar to view a list of recent actions. Use the Redo feature if you change your mind after clicking Undo. Some actions (such as Save) cannot be reversed with Undo.

PROJECT: You will continue to edit the quotation for Marquee Productions by inserting and deleting cells.

STEPS

1 With Excel S2-01 open, select the range A24:A25.

In the next two steps you will insert cells to add two entries between *Soup and salad* and *Hot entrée*.

2 Click Insert and then Cells.

PROBLEM? Don't see Cells on the Insert menu? Click the double down-pointing arrows at the bottom of the menu, click Insert a second time, or simply wait a few seconds—the menu will expand to show additional options.

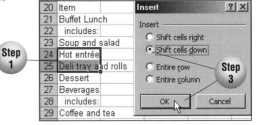

3 At the Insert dialog box, click Shift cells down and then click OK.

4 Click A24, key **Vegetable tray with dip**, and then press Enter.

5 Key **Seafood hors d'oeuvres** and then press Enter.

6 Make A32 the active cell.

7 Click Edit and then Delete.

8 At the Delete dialog box, make sure Shift cells up is selected, then click OK.

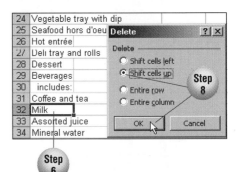

9 Look at C27:G27, C33:G33, C39:G39, and G41. The values for *Beverages, Snacks, Delivery,* and *Total* no longer appear beside the correct labels. This is because we did not insert or delete *entire rows.* You can correct the worksheet with Undo.

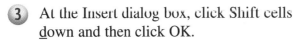

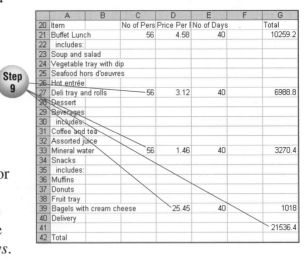

10   Click the Undo button 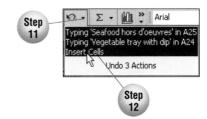 on the Standard toolbar.

      The last action, deleting A32, is reversed.

11   Click the down-pointing triangle to the right of the Undo button.

12   Point to *Insert Cells* and then click the left mouse button.

> **PROBLEM?**
>
> Your Undo list may not coincide with these steps if you have edited the worksheet beyond the steps in this topic. You can preserve your editing by not using Undo—insert and delete rows as needed.

Step 11

Step 12

13   Make A43 the active cell.

14   Click Insert and then Cells.

15   At the Insert dialog box, click OK.

      A new cell is inserted and the existing text in A43 is moved down to A44.

16   Key **Quotation is valid for 30 days** and then press Enter.

17   Click Undo.

18   Click Edit and then Redo Typing.

      Redo reverses the action of Undo.

19   Save Excel S2-01.

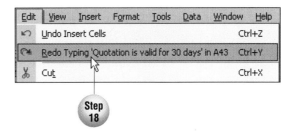

Step 18

In Addition

More about Undo

Some actions cannot be undone. For example, if you click the Save button on the Standard toolbar, Undo will not be available to reverse the save operation. If the action you have completed is not reversible, the Undo button on the Edit menu will be dimmed and the option will read, *Can't Undo*.

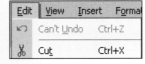

IN BRIEF

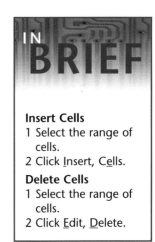

Insert Cells
1 Select the range of cells.
2 Click Insert, Cells.

Delete Cells
1 Select the range of cells.
2 Click Edit, Delete.

2.3 Inserting, Deleting, Hiding, and Unhiding Columns and Rows

Rows and columns can be inserted or deleted using options from the Insert and Edit menus, or from the shortcut menu. Context-sensitive shortcut menus display when you right-click the mouse over a selected area. A row or column can be hidden from the worksheet display. The data is removed from view but is not deleted. You might want to do this if the worksheet contains confidential information; hidden rows or columns do not print. Redisplay hidden data by unhiding the rows or columns.

PROJECT: You will add to and delete items from the quotation in the previous topic by inserting and deleting rows. The information in columns I through K is confidential profit data. You want to hide these columns so the printout of the quotation does not display them.

S T E P S

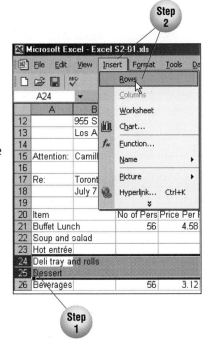

① With Excel S2-01 open, position the cell pointer (displays as a right-pointing black arrow) over row indicator *24*, hold down the left mouse button, and then drag the mouse down over *25*.

> This selects rows 24 and 25. Inserted rows are placed *above* the selected rows and columns are inserted to the *left*.

② Click Insert and then Rows.

> Two blank rows are inserted. All rows below the inserted rows are shifted down.

③ Click A24, key **Vegetable tray with dip**, and then press Enter.

④ Key **Seafood hors d'oeuvres** and then press Enter.

⑤ Select row 32.

⑥ Click Edit and then Delete.

> The data in row 32 is removed from the worksheet. All rows below the deleted row shift up to fill in the space.

⑦ Select row 22. Hold down Ctrl and then select rows 30 and 35.

> Hold down the Ctrl key to select multiple rows or columns that are not adjacent.

⑧ Position the pointer within any of the three selected rows, *right*-click to display the shortcut menu, and then click Delete.

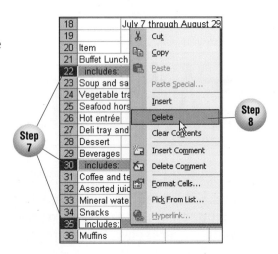

(9) Select column F and display the shortcut menu by positioning the cell pointer over column indicator letter *F* and *right*-clicking the mouse.

(10) At the shortcut menu, click <u>D</u>elete.

> Data in columns to the right of the deleted column are shifted left to fill in the space.

(11) Position the cell pointer (displays as a down-pointing black arrow) over column indicator letter *H*, hold down the left mouse button, and drag the mouse right over *J*.

(12) Click F<u>o</u>rmat, point to <u>C</u>olumn, and then click H<u>i</u>de.

> Columns H, I, and J are now hidden. Notice the column letter indicators are now A through G, and then K and onward.

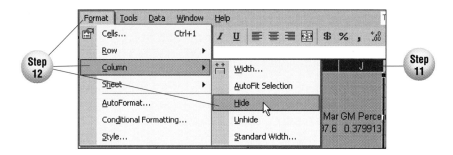

(13) Make F11 the active cell, key **November 21, 2002**, and then press Enter.

> Excel displays dates in the format *dd-mmm-yy* (21-Nov-02).

(14) Save Excel S2-01.

In Addition

Redisplaying Hidden Columns

To redisplay hidden data, select the column or row before and after the hidden data and then click F<u>o</u>rmat, point to <u>R</u>ow or <u>C</u>olumn, and click <u>U</u>nhide. For example, to redisplay the columns hidden in step 12, you would select columns G and K.

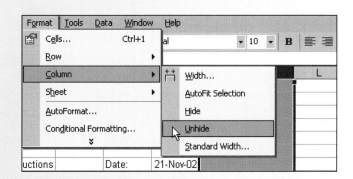

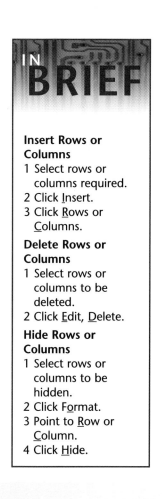

IN BRIEF

Insert Rows or Columns
1 Select rows or columns required.
2 Click <u>I</u>nsert.
3 Click <u>R</u>ows or <u>C</u>olumns.

Delete Rows or Columns
1 Select rows or columns to be deleted.
2 Click <u>E</u>dit, <u>D</u>elete.

Hide Rows or Columns
1 Select rows or columns to be hidden.
2 Click F<u>o</u>rmat.
3 Point to <u>R</u>ow or <u>C</u>olumn.
4 Click H<u>i</u>de.

2.4 Moving and Copying Cells

You learned how to use copy and paste to copy formulas in the payroll worksheet for The Waterfront Bistro. You can also use cut and paste to move the contents of a cell or range of cells to another location in the worksheet. The selected cells being cut or copied are called the *source*. The cell or range of cells that is receiving the source data is called the *destination*. If data already exists in the destination cells, Excel will replace the contents in the destination location.

PROJECT: In further changes to your catering quotation, you will move text in the quotation and duplicate the price per person from beverages to snacks by copying the cell containing the price.

STEPS

① With Excel S2-01 open, make E3 the active cell.

② Click the Cut button on the Standard toolbar.

> A moving marquee surrounds the source after you use Cut or Copy, indicating the cell contents have been placed in the Clipboard.

PROBLEM **?** Can't find the Cut button? Click the Toolbar Options button in the middle of the toolbar (just left of the Font button) to display more Standard toolbar buttons in a drop-down palette.

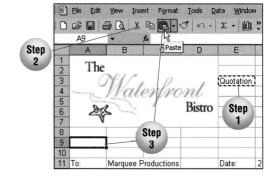

③ Make A9 the active cell and then click the Paste button on the Standard toolbar.

> The text *Quotation* is removed from E3 and placed in A9. In the next step you will move a range of cells using a method called *drag and drop*.

④ Select the range A17:B18.

> You are only selecting to column B since the entries *Toronto Location Filming* and *July 7 through August 29, 2003* are stored in B17 and B18, respectively.

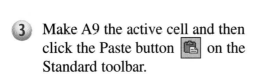

⑤ Point at any one of the four borders surrounding the selected range.

> When you point at a border, the pointer changes from the thick white cross to a white arrow with the move icon attached to it (four-headed arrow).

⑥ Hold down the left mouse button, drag the top left corner of the range to E15, and then release the mouse.

> A gray border will appear as you drag, indicating the placement of the range when you release the mouse. The destination range displays in a yellow box below the gray border.

7 Make D28 the active cell.

8 Click the Copy button 📋 on the Standard toolbar.

9 Make D32 the active cell, and then click the Paste button 📋 on the Standard toolbar.

> The existing data in D32 is replaced with the value copied from D28 and the Paste Options button appears. The moving marquee remains around D28. The moving marquee will disappear when you perform another action or press Esc. Cells cut or copied to the Clipboard can be pasted more than once in the active workbook, in another workbook, or in another Office application.

Steps 7–8

26	Deli tray and rolls		
27	Dessert		
28	Beverages	56	3.12
29	Coffee and tea		
30	Assorted juice		
31	Mineral water		
32	Snacks	56	3.12
33	Muffins		
34	Donuts		

Step 9

Paste Options Button

10 Press Esc to remove the moving marquee from D28.

11 Make A23 the active cell.

12 Point at any one of the four borders surrounding A23 until the pointer displays as a white arrow with the move icon attached to it, hold down Ctrl, and then drag the mouse to A36. Release the mouse button first, and then release the Ctrl key.

> When you hold down Ctrl while dragging, a plus sign appears attached to the pointer, indicating the source contents are being *copied*.

22	Soup and salad
23	Vegetable tray with dip
24	Seafood hors d'oeuvres
25	Hot entrée
26	Deli tray and rolls
27	Dessert
28	Beverages
29	Coffee and tea
30	Assorted juice
31	Mineral water
32	Snacks
33	Muffins
34	Donuts
35	Fruit tray
36	Vegetable tray with dip
37	Delivery

Step 12

13 Save Excel S2-01.

In Addition

Relative and Absolute Addressing

When you used copy and paste to copy formulas in the payroll worksheet for The Waterfront Bistro, the cell addresses in the formula were changed *relative* to the destination row or column. In some cases you will want a cell address in a formula to remain fixed when it is copied. This is referred to as *absolute* addressing. A cell address can be made absolute by inserting a dollar symbol ($) in front of the column letter or row number that you do not want changed. Following are some examples of ways to insert absolute cell addresses in a formula that will be copied.

=$A$12*.01   Neither the column nor the row will change
=$A12*.01   The column will remain fixed but the row will change
=A$12*.01   The column will change but the row will remain fixed

In Brief

Move Cells
1 Select the source cells.
2 Click Cut.
3 Select the destination cells.
4 Click Paste.

Copy Cells
1 Select the source cells.
2 Click Copy.
3 Select the destination cells.
4 Click Paste.

2.5 Adjusting Column Width and Row Height

By default, columns are all the same width and rows are all the same height. Columns are initially set to the average number of digits 0 through 9 that can fit in a cell in the standard font. In some cases you do not have to increase the width when the text is too wide for the column, since labels "spill over" into the next cell if it is empty. Some column headings in the quotation are truncated because an entry exists in the column immediately to the right. Excel automatically adjusts the height of rows to accommodate the size of the text within the cells. Increasing the row height adds more space between rows, which can be used as a design technique to draw attention to a series of cells.

PROJECT: To make sure Marquee Productions will understand all of the items in your quotation, you will adjust the column widths for columns in which the entire label is not currently visible and increase the height of the row containing the column headings.

STEPS

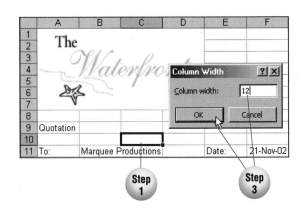

Step 1

Step 3

1. With Excel S2-01 open, make any cell in column C the active cell.

2. Click Format, point to Column, and then click Width.

3. At the Column Width dialog box, key **12** and then click OK or press Enter.

   In the next step you will adjust the width of column D using the mouse.

4. Position the mouse pointer on the boundary line in the column indicator row between columns D and E until the pointer changes to a vertical line with a left- and right-pointing arrow ⬌.

5. Hold down the left mouse button, drag the boundary line to the right until *Width: 14.29 (105 pixels)* displays in the yellow box, and then release the mouse button.

   As you drag the boundary line to the right or left, a dotted line appears in the column in the worksheet area indicating the new width.

   Step 5

6. Position the mouse pointer on the boundary line in the column indicator row between columns E and F until the pointer changes to a vertical line with a left- and right-pointing arrow, and then double-click the left mouse button.

   Double-clicking the boundary line sets the width to fit the length of the longest entry within the column, referred to as *AutoFit*. If, after decreasing a column width, cells that previously had values in them now display as a series of pound symbols (########), the column is now too narrow. Widen the column to redisplay the values.

7. Increase the width of column B to 12.00 (89 pixels).

   After reviewing the worksheet you decide all of the columns with numeric values should be the same width. In the next steps you will learn how to set the width of multiple columns.

8 Position the mouse pointer on column indicator letter *C*, hold down the left mouse button, and then drag the mouse right to column F.

> This selects columns C through F.

9 Position the mouse pointer on *any* of the right boundary lines within the selected range of columns until the pointer changes to a vertical line with a left- and right-pointing arrow.

> Any changes made to the width will affect all of the selected columns.

10 Drag the boundary line to the right until *Width: 15.00 (110 pixels)* displays in the yellow box, and then release the mouse button.

11 Click in any cell to deselect the columns.

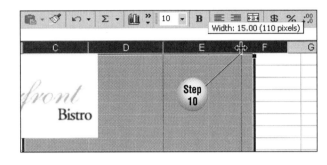

12 Move E15:F16 to A17:B18. Refer to topic 2.4 if you need assistance with this step.

> In the next steps you will adjust row height using the mouse.

13 Position the mouse pointer on the boundary line below row 20 until the pointer changes to a horizontal line with an up- and down-pointing arrow.

14 Drag the boundary line down until *Height: 19.50 (26 pixels)* displays in the yellow box, and then release the mouse button.

15 Save Excel S2-01.

In Addition

Row Height Dialog Box

A similar sequence of steps that you used for adjusting column width using the Column Width dialog box can be used to increase or decrease the height of a row with the Row Height dialog box, shown at the right. Click any cell within the row, click F*o*rmat, point to R*o*w, and then click H*e*ight. Key the desired height and press Enter or click OK.

Increase or Decrease Column Width
1 Select column(s).
2 Click F*o*rmat.
3 Point to *C*olumn.
4 Click *W*idth.
5 Key desired width.
6 Click OK.

Increase or Decrease Row Height
1 Select row(s).
2 Click F*o*rmat.
3 Point to *R*ow.
4 Click H*e*ight.
5 Key desired height.
6 Click OK.

Adjust Width or Height Using Mouse
1 Select column(s) or row(s).
2 Drag the boundary to the right of the column or below the row.

2.6 Freezing and Unfreezing Panes; Changing the Zoom

When you scroll to the right or down to view parts of a worksheet that do not fit in the current window, some column or row headings may scroll off the screen making it difficult for you to relate to the text or values. The Freeze Panes option from the Window menu will cause rows and columns to remain fixed when you scroll. All rows above and to the left of the active cell are frozen. You can magnify or reduce the display by changing the settings in the Zoom dialog box. By default, the worksheet displays at 100%. You can choose from predefined magnification settings or enter a value between 10 and 400 in the Custom box. Changing the magnification does not affect printing since worksheets are printed at 100% unless you change the scaling in Page Setup.

PROJECT: You will freeze column and row headings in the quotation to facilitate scrolling and reduce the zoom percentage to view more cells at the same time.

STEPS

1. With Excel S2-01 open, make A21 the active cell.

2. Click <u>W</u>indow and then <u>F</u>reeze Panes.

   All rows above the active cell are frozen. A black line appears below row 20 to indicate which rows will remain fixed when scrolling.

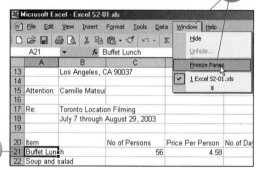

3. Scroll down the worksheet to the end of the quotation.

   Notice rows 1 through 20 do not scroll off the screen.

4. Click <u>W</u>indow and then Un<u>f</u>reeze Panes.

   The <u>F</u>reeze Panes option changes to Un<u>f</u>reeze Panes when rows or columns have been frozen.

5. Position the mouse pointer on column indicator letter *G*, hold down the left mouse button, and then drag the mouse right to column K.

   This selects columns G through K. The yellow box indicates that five columns are selected (columns H through J are hidden).

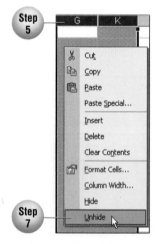

6. Position the mouse pointer within the selected columns and *right*-click.

7. Click <u>U</u>nhide at the shortcut menu.

   This redisplays hidden columns H through J.

8. Make C21 the active cell, click <u>W</u>indow and then <u>F</u>reeze Panes.

   Rows 1 through 20 and columns A and B are frozen.

PROBLEM **?**
If the wrong cell was active, click <u>W</u>indow and then Un<u>f</u>reeze Panes. Make the correct cell active and then refreeze the panes.

9 Scroll right and down the worksheet until you can see J42.

Black horizontal and vertical lines indicate which columns and rows are frozen, as shown in Figure E2.1.

FIGURE E2.1 Lines Showing Frozen Rows and Columns

17	Re:	Toronto Locatic						
18		July 7 through						
19								
20	Item		No of Days	Total		Our Cost	Gross Mar	GM Percent
39	Total			25254.8			11248.4	0.445397
40								
41	Quotation is valid for 30 da							
42	Note: All prices are tax inc							
43								

Horizontal and vertical lines indicate which rows and columns are frozen.

10 Click View and then Zoom.

11 At the Zoom dialog box, click 75% and then click OK.

The worksheet is reduced to 75% magnification, allowing you to view more columns and rows. The worksheet can be edited at any Zoom setting.

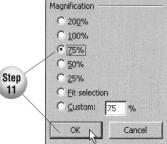

Step 11

12 Select columns H through J and then double-click any of the column boundary lines at the right within the selected range of columns to change the width to AutoFit.

13 Click in any cell to deselect the columns, click View, and then click Zoom.

14 At the Zoom dialog box, click 100% and then click OK.

15 Save Excel S2-01.

In Addition

Splitting the Window

As an alternative to freezing panes, you can split the window to view two parts of a worksheet at the same time. (A window cannot be split if Freeze Panes is activated.) The window can be split horizontally, vertically, or both. To do this, point at the Split box located at the top of the vertical scroll bar until the split pointer appears ⬌ and then drag the split box down to the position you want the split to occur. A split box is also located at the left edge of the horizontal scroll bar. To remove the split, drag the split box back up to the top of the window. The difference between splitting the window and freezing panes is that with a split window you have two sets of scroll bars so that you can scroll to different parts of the same worksheet.

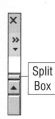

Split Box

IN BRIEF

Freeze Panes
1 Make the cell active below and right of the row or column headings you want to freeze.
2 Click Window, Freeze Panes.

Change Zoom Setting
1 Click View, Zoom.
2 Choose a magnification setting.
3 Click OK.

2.7 Changing the Font, Size, Style, and Color of Cells

The *font* is the typeface used to display and print data. The default font in Excel is Arial, but several other fonts are available. The size of the font is measured in units called *points*. A point is approximately 1/72 of an inch measured vertically. The default font size used by Excel is 10-point. The larger the point size, the larger the type. Each font's style can be changed to display in **bold**, *italic*, or ***bold italic***. Text in cells displays in black with a white background. You can add emphasis or interest to the worksheet by changing the color of the text or the color of the background.

PROJECT: To add to the visual appeal of your quotation, you will change the font and font size, and apply attributes such as bold and color to the text *Quotation*.

STEPS

1 With Excel S2-01 open, click <u>T</u>ools and then <u>C</u>ustomize.

> Completing the remaining steps in this topic will be easier if you can see all of the buttons on the Formatting toolbar. In the next step, you will display the Standard and Formatting toolbars as two rows. Skip steps 1 and 2 if your Standard and Formatting toolbars are already separated.

2 If necessary, click the <u>O</u>ptions tab in the Customize dialog box. Click the <u>S</u>how Standard and Formatting toolbars on two rows check box, and then click Close.

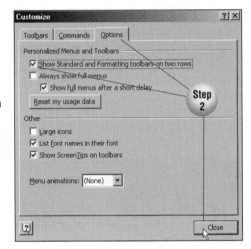

3 Make A9 the active cell.

4 Click the down-pointing triangle next to the Font button on the Formatting toolbar, scroll down the list of fonts, and then click *Times New Roman*.

> The list of fonts on your system may vary.

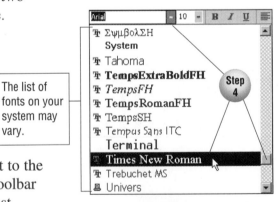

5 Click the down-pointing triangle next to the Font Size button on the Formatting toolbar and then click *18* in the drop-down list.

> The row height is automatically increased to accommodate the larger type size.

6 Click the Bold button **B** on the Formatting toolbar.

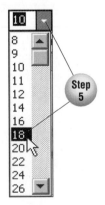

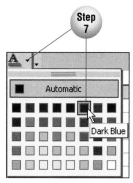

(7) Click the down-pointing triangle next to the Font Color button on the Formatting toolbar and then click Dark Blue in the color palette.

(8) Select A9:F9 and then click the Merge and Center button on the Formatting toolbar.

(9) With A9:F9 still selected, click the down-pointing triangle next to the Fill Color button on the Formatting toolbar and then click Light Turquoise in the color palette.

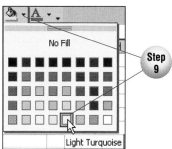

> Fill is the color of the background in the cell. Changing the fill color is sometimes referred to as *shading* a cell.

(10) Make A39 the active cell.

(11) Hold down Ctrl and then click F39.

> This selects both A39 and F39.

(12) Click the Bold button and the Italic button I on the Formatting toolbar.

> More than one attribute can be applied to a cell.

(13) Click in any cell to deselect A39 and F39.

(14) Save Excel S2-01.

In Addition

Format Cells

The Format Cells dialog box with the Font tab selected (shown below) can be used to change the font, font size, font style, and color of text. Additional style options such as Underline are available, as well as special effects options such as Strikethrough, Superscript, and Subscript. Select the cells you want to change, click Format and then Cells. Click the Font tab in the Format Cells dialog box and then change the required options.

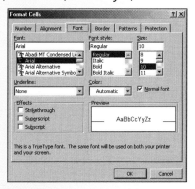

2.8 Formatting Numeric Cells; Adjusting Decimal Places

In the payroll worksheet for The Waterfront Bistro, you learned how to format numeric cells to the Currency format which added a dollar symbol ($), comma in the thousands, and two decimal places to each value. Other numeric formats include Comma, Percent, and Accounting. By default, cells are initially set to the *General* format. The General format has no specific numeric style. The number of decimal places in a selected range of cells can be increased or decreased using the Increase Decimal and Decrease Decimal buttons on the Formatting toolbar.

PROJECT: Apply the Accounting, Comma, and Percent formats to the numeric cells within the quotation using buttons from the Formatting toolbar and the Format Cells dialog box.

S·T·E·P·S

① With Excel S2-01 open, click Window and then Unfreeze Panes.

② Click View and Zoom.

③ At the Zoom dialog box, click Custom, key **85** in the % text box, and then click OK.

Unfreezing the panes and reducing the zoom percentage will allow you to work with a larger range of cells in the window.

④ Scroll up or down until rows 20 through 40 are visible in the window.

⑤ Make F21 the active cell.

⑥ Hold down Ctrl and then click I21, F39, and I39.

⑦ Click Format and then Cells.

⑧ If necessary, click the Number tab in the Format Cells dialog box, click *Accounting* in the Category list box, and then click OK.

A preview of the selected cell with the format applied appears in the Sample box. If necessary, the number of decimal places and the currency symbol can be changed before you click OK.

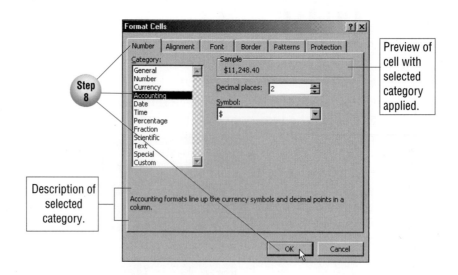

Step 8

Description of selected category.

Preview of cell with selected category applied.

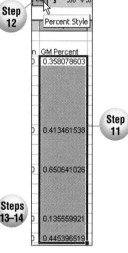

9 Select F28, I28, F32, I32, F37, and I37.

10 Click the Comma Style button [,] on the Formatting toolbar.

> Comma Style formats cells the same as the Accounting format with the exception of the Currency symbol.

11 Select J21:J39.

12 Click the Percent Style button [%] on the Formatting toolbar.

> Percent Style causes Excel to multiply cell values by 100 and add a percent symbol (%) to the end of each result in the selected range.

13 With the range J21:J39 still selected, click the Increase Decimal button [.00 →] twice on the Formatting toolbar.

> One decimal place is added to or removed from the cells in the selected range each time you click Increase Decimal or Decrease Decimal.

14 With the range J21:J39 still selected, click the Decrease Decimal button [← .00] once on the Formatting toolbar.

15 Make H37 the active cell and then click the Increase Decimal button twice to display two decimal places.

16 Change the zoom percentage back to 100%.

17 Save Excel S2-01.

Our Cost	Gross Margin	GM Percent
2.94	$ 3,673.60	35.8%
1.83	2,889.60	41.3%
1.09	4,547.20	65.1%
22.00	138.00	13.6%
	$ 11,248.40	44.5%

In Addition

Styles

A *style* is a group of formats saved under a style name. Once a style has been defined, you can apply the group of formats by selecting the style name from a list of styles. A style is useful if you frequently apply a particular font, alignment, and numeric format to cells. To create a new style or modify an existing style, select a cell that already has the formats applied that you want to save, and click Format and then Style. At the Style dialog box (shown at the right), key a name for the style in the Style name box or select one of the predefined style names to edit an existing style, and then click OK.

IN BRIEF

Change Numeric Format Using Toolbar
1 Select cells.
2 Click style button on Formatting toolbar.
3 Deselect cells.

Change Numeric Format Using Format Cells
1 Select cells.
2 Click Format, Cells.
3 Click Number tab.
4 Select desired format in Category list.
5 If necessary, change Decimal places, Symbol, or Negative numbers options.
6 Click OK.
7 Deselect cells.

EXCEL

2.9 Changing the Alignment and Indentation of Cells

Data in a cell can be left aligned, right aligned, or centered within the column. A heading or title that you want to position over several columns can be merged and then the text within the merged cell can be aligned at the left, center, or right. Data can be indented from the left edge of the cell or rotated to add visual interest.

PROJECT: Change the alignment of column headings and values, and indent labels from the left edge of column A to improve the appearance of the quotation.

STEPS

1. With Excel S2-01 open, edit the column headings in C20 and E20 to include a period (.) after the abbreviation for *Number*. For example, the edited column heading in C20 will be *No. of Persons*.

2. Select C20:J20.

3. Click the Center button ≡ on the Formatting toolbar.

4. Select C21, C28, and C32 and then center them within the column.

5. Center the entries in column E.

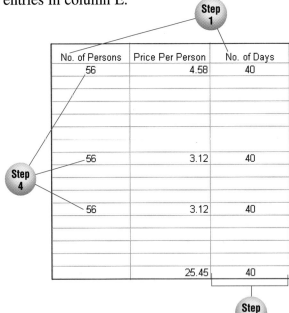

6. Select A22:A27.

7. Click the Increase Indent button ⬚ on the Formatting toolbar.

   Each time you click Increase Indent, the contents of the selected cells are indented by approximately one character width. If you click Increase Indent one too many times, click the Decrease Indent button ⬚ to return the text to the previous indent position.

8 Select A29:A31 and then click Increase Indent.

9 Select A33:A36 and then click Increase Indent.

10 Select A20:F20 and then bold the cells.

11 Make F11 the active cell and then click the Align Left button ▤ on the Formatting toolbar.

> By default, Excel aligns date entries at the right edge of a column since dates are converted to a serial number and treated in a similar manner to values. You will learn more about using dates in Excel in a later topic.

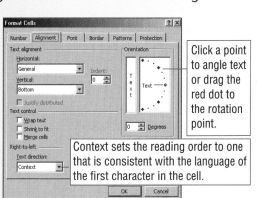

Quotation

To:	Marquee Productions		Date:	21-Nov-02		Step 11
	955 South Alameda Street					
	Los Angeles, CA 90037					
Attention:	Camille Matsui					
Re:	Toronto Location Filming					
	July 7 through August 29, 2003					
Item		**No. of Persons**	**Price Per Person**	**No. of Days**	**Total**	Step 10
Buffet Lunch		56	4.58	40	$ 10,259.20	

12 Save Excel S2-01.

In Addition

Rotating, Vertical Alignment, and Text Controls

The Alignment tab in the Format Cells dialog box (shown below) contains options to rotate text, align text vertically, control the length of labels within a cell, and designate the reading order for text. To rotate text, select the cells you want to rotate and then display the Format Cells dialog box with the Alignment tab selected. Click the point in the Orientation box at which you want the text to be angled, or drag the red dot to the desired angle.

The options available from the Vertical drop-down list are Center, Bottom, Justify, and Distributed. Use the Wrap text, Shrink to fit, and Merge cells options in the Text control section to format long labels. Options under Text direction include Context, Left-to-Right, or Right-to-Left.

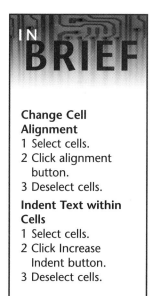

Click a point to angle text or drag the red dot to the rotation point.

Context sets the reading order to one that is consistent with the language of the first character in the cell.

IN BRIEF

Change Cell Alignment
1 Select cells.
2 Click alignment button.
3 Deselect cells.

Indent Text within Cells
1 Select cells.
2 Click Increase Indent button.
3 Deselect cells.

2.10 Adding Borders and Shading; Autoformatting

Borders in various styles and colors can be applied to display and print in selected cells within the worksheet. Borders can be added to the top, left, bottom, or right edge of a cell. Use borders to underscore headings or totals, or to emphasize other cells. Shading adds color and/or a pattern to the background of a cell. Excel's AutoFormat feature includes several predefined worksheet format settings. In the AutoFormat dialog box you can scroll through samples of the predefined autoformats and select a style that suits your worksheet.

PROJECT: To complete your presentation, you will add borders, shading, and a pattern to cells, and apply an autoformat to the quotation.

S T E P S

1. With Excel S2-01 open, hide columns H through J.

2. Click the down-pointing triangle next to the Zoom button on the Standard toolbar and then click 75% in the drop-down list.

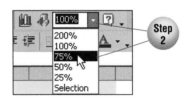

Step 2

3. Select A20:F20.

   In the next steps you will add a border to the top and bottom of the column headings using the Borders button on the Formatting toolbar.

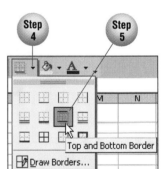

Step 4   Step 5

4. Click the down-pointing triangle to the right of the Borders button ▦ ▾ on the Formatting toolbar.

   A palette of border style options displays. Click a border style to add the border to the selected cells. The most recently selected border style displays in the Borders button. To apply the same border style to another cell, select the cell and then click the Borders button.

5. Click the Top and Bottom Border button (third from left in second row).

6. Click in any cell to deselect the range A20:F20 and view the border.

7. Make F39 the active cell.

   In the next steps you will add a double underline border to the bottom of F39 using options in the Format Cells dialog box.

8. Click Format and then Cells.

(9) Click the Border tab in the Format Cells dialog box.

(10) Click the double line in the Style box (last option in second column), click the Bottom border button in the Border section, and then click OK.

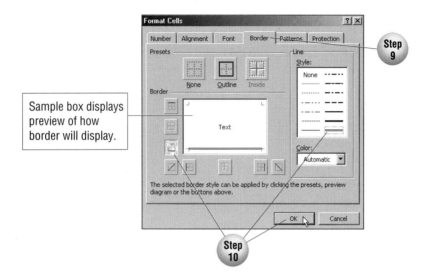

Sample box displays preview of how border will display.

Step 9

Step 10

(11) Click in another cell in the worksheet so you can view the double bottom border in F39.

(12) Select A20:F20.

In the next steps you will use the Patterns tab in the Format Cells dialog box to add shading color to cells. The Format Cells dialog box provides more color choices than the Fill Color palette as well as including various patterns that can be placed in the background.

(13) Click Format and then Cells.

(14) Click the Patterns tab in the Format Cells dialog box.

(15) Click the Pale Yellow color button (third from left in second row from bottom).

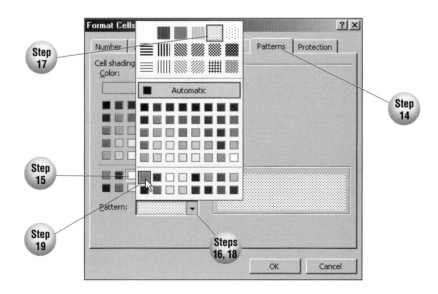

Step 17

Step 14

Step 15

Step 19

Steps 16, 18

(continued)

(16) Click the down-pointing triangle next to the <u>P</u>attern box.

> This displays the Pattern style and color palette.

(17) Click 12.5% Gray (fifth from left in first row of patterns).

(18) Click the down-pointing triangle next to the <u>P</u>attern box.

(19) Click the Periwinkle color button (first from left in second row from bottom).

(20) Click OK and then click in any cell to deselect the range and view the shading and pattern.

(21) Change the zoom back to 100%.

(22) Save and then print Excel S2-01.

(23) Select A20:F39.

(24) Click <u>F</u>ormat and then <u>A</u>utoFormat.

(25) Scroll down the AutoFormat list box until you can see the Colorful 2 style.

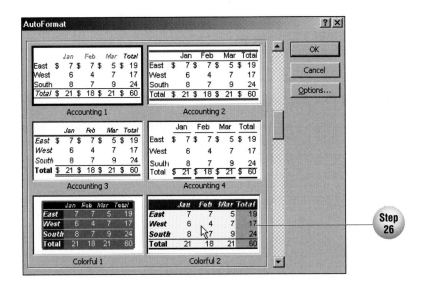

(26) Double-click *Colorful 2*.

> The Colorful 2 style is applied to the selected cells. Any formats already applied to the selected cells are overwritten with the Colorful 2 format settings. Single-click an autoformat and then click the <u>O</u>ptions button in the AutoFormat dialog box to expand the dialog box and deselect individual formats. The autoformat options that can be individually disabled include: <u>N</u>umber, <u>B</u>order, <u>F</u>ont, <u>P</u>atterns, <u>A</u>lignment, and <u>W</u>idth/Height.

27 Click in any cell to deselect the range and then print the worksheet.

If you are printing on a printer other than a color printer, the cells with color and shading applied to them are printed in shades of gray. Autoformats such as Colorful 2 may not be suitable for black and white printing.

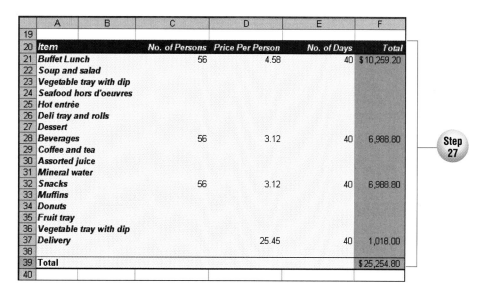

	A	B	C	D	E	F
19						
20	*Item*		*No. of Persons*	*Price Per Person*	*No. of Days*	*Total*
21	Buffet Lunch		56	4.58	40	$10,259.20
22	Soup and salad					
23	Vegetable tray with dip					
24	Seafood hors d'oeuvres					
25	Hot entrée					
26	Deli tray and rolls					
27	Dessert					
28	Beverages		56	3.12	40	6,988.80
29	Coffee and tea					
30	Assorted juice					
31	Mineral water					
32	Snacks		56	3.12	40	6,988.80
33	Muffins					
34	Donuts					
35	Fruit tray					
36	Vegetable tray with dip					
37	Delivery			25.45	40	1,018.00
38						
39	Total					$25,254.80
40						

Step 27

28 Click File and then Save As.

29 Key **Excel S2-02** in the File name text box and then click Save.

In Addition

Copying Formats with Format Painter

The Format Painter button ![brush] on the Standard toolbar can be used to copy formats from an existing cell to other cells in the worksheet. Activate the cell containing the desired formats and then click the Format Painter button. The cell pointer displays with a paintbrush attached to it. Select the cell or range of cells to which you want the formats copied. The formats are copied to the cells and Format Painter is automatically turned off. Double-clicking the Format Painter button will turn on Format Painter for consecutive copying until you turn the feature off by clicking the Format Painter button to deactivate it.

IN BRIEF

Add Borders
1 Select cells.
2 Click Format, Cells.
3 Click Border tab.
4 Select Border options.
5 Deselect cells.

Add Shading/Patterns
1 Select cells.
2 Click Format, Cells.
3 Click Patterns tab.
4 Select shading options.
5 Deselect cells.

Autoformat a Worksheet
1 Select cells.
2 Click Format, AutoFormat.
3 Double-click desired autoformat style.
4 Deselect cells.

2.11 Using Find and Replace

Use the Find command to search for specific labels or values that you want to verify or edit. The Find command will move to each cell containing the text you specify. The Replace command will search for a label, value, or format and automatically replace it with another label, value, or format. The Find and Replace feature ensures that all occurrences of the specified text are included.

PROJECT: Use Find to review the cells containing the value 3.12 (the price quoted for beverages and snacks). An e-mail from Camille Matsui of Marquee Productions has just arrived to advise you that the film crew will require catering services for three additional days. Use the Replace command to correct the number of days. Finally, you will use the Replace command to change all cells that are currently set in bold and italic to the regular font style.

STEPS

① With Excel S2-02 open, press Ctrl + Home to make cell A1 active.

② Click Edit and then Find.

③ Key **3.12** in the Find what text box and then click Find Next.

> The cell containing the first occurrence of *3.12* becomes active.

PROBLEM ?

Can't see the active cell? Drag the Find dialog box out of the way if it is obscuring your view of the worksheet.

Step 3

Step 6

④ Click Find Next.

> The cell containing the next occurrence of *3.12* becomes active.

> The active cell moves to the next occurrence of the specified text each time you click Find Next.

⑤ Click Find Next.

> The cell containing the first occurrence of *3.12* becomes active since there are only two occurrences.

⑥ Click the Close button to close the Find dialog box.

> In this example the Find command was used to find only two occurrences that were both visible within the current window. In a large worksheet with many rows and columns of data, the Find command is a very efficient method of moving to a specific cell.

⑦ Click Edit and then Replace.

> Notice the previous entry that was searched for (3.12) appears in the Find what text box.

⑧ Drag to select *3.12* in the Find what text box and then key **40**.

⑨ Press Tab to move the insertion point to the Replace with text box and then key **43**.

⑩ Click Replace All.

> Excel will search through the entire worksheet and automatically change all occurrences of *40* to *43*.

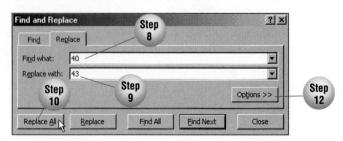

EXCEL

56

⑪ Click OK at the message that Excel has completed the search and has made 4 replacements.

⑫ With the Find and Replace dialog box still open, click the Options button.

⑬ Drag to select *40* in the Find what text box and then press Delete. Drag to select *43* in the Replace with text box and then press Delete.

⑭ Click the Format button at the right of the Find what text box.

⑮ If necessary, click the Font tab in the Find Format dialog box. Click *Bold Italic* in the Font style section and then click OK.

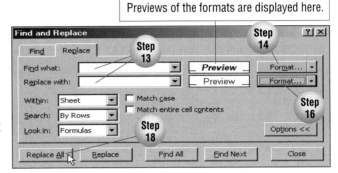

Previews of the formats are displayed here.

A preview of the format that will be searched for displays between the Find what text box and the Format button.

⑯ Click the Format button at the right of the Replace with text box.

⑰ Click *Regular* in the Font style section and then click OK.

A preview of the format that will be replaced for each occurrence of the found format displays between the Replace with text box and the Format button.

⑱ Click Replace All.

⑲ Click OK at the message that Excel has completed its search and has made 42 replacements.

⑳ Click the down-pointing triangle next to the Format button at the right of Find what and then click Clear Find Format.

㉑ Click the down-pointing triangle next to the Format button at the right of Replace with and then click Clear Replace Format.

㉒ Click the Options button.

㉓ Click the Close button in the Find and Replace dialog box.

㉔ Save, print, and then close Excel S2-02.

Clear formats after a Replace operation.

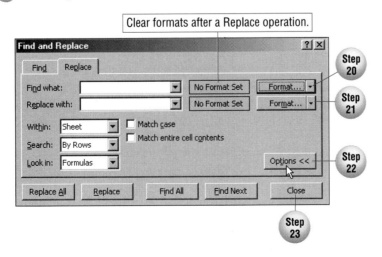

Find a Label or Value
1 Click Edit, Find.
2 Key the label or value in Find what text box.
3 Click Find Next.

Replace a Label or Value
1 Click Edit, Replace.
2 Key label or value in Find what text box.
3 Key replacement label or value in Replace with text box.
4 Click Find Next or Replace All.

EXCEL

FEATURES SUMMARY

Feature	Button	Menu	Keyboard
Accounting Format		Format, Cells, Number	Ctrl + 1
AutoFormat		Format, AutoFormat	
Bold	**B**	Format, Cells, Font	Ctrl + B
Borders		Format, Cells, Border	Ctrl + 1
Center		Format, Cells, Alignment	Ctrl + 1
Clear Cell		Edit, Clear, All	
Clear Cell Contents		Edit, Clear, Contents	Delete
Clear Cell Formats		Edit, Clear, Formats	
Column Width		Format, Column, Width	
Comma Style	,	Format, Style, Style name	
Copy		Edit, Copy	Ctrl + C
Cut		Edit, Cut	Ctrl + X
Decrease Decimal		Format, Cells, Number	Ctrl + 1
Decrease Indent		Format, Cells, Alignment	Ctrl + 1
Delete Cells		Edit, Delete	
Delete Column or Row		Edit, Delete	
Fill Color/Shading		Format, Cells, Patterns	Ctrl + 1
Find		Edit, Find	Ctrl + F
Font	Arial	Format, Cells, Font	Ctrl + 1
Font Color	A	Format, Cells, Font	Ctrl + 1
Font Size	10	Format, Cells, Font	Ctrl + 1
Freeze Panes		Window, Freeze Panes	
Hide Column or Row		Format, Row or Column, Hide	
Increase Decimal		Format, Cells, Number	Ctrl + 1
Increase Indent		Format, Cells, Alignment	Ctrl + 1
Insert Cells		Insert, Cells	
Insert Column or Row		Insert, Columns or Rows	
Italic	*I*	Format, Cells, Font	Ctrl + 1
Left Align		Format, Cells, Alignment	Ctrl + 1
Paste		Edit, Paste	Ctrl + V

Feature	Button	Menu	Keyboard
Percent Style	%	Format, Style, Style name	
Redo	↻	Edit, Redo	Ctrl + Y
Replace		Edit, Replace	Ctrl + H
Right Align	≡	Format, Cells, Alignment	Ctrl + 1
Row Height		Format, Row, Height	
Spell Check	ABC✓	Tools, Spelling	F7
Undo	↺	Edit, Undo	Ctrl + Z
Unfreeze Panes		Window, Unfreeze Panes	
Unhide Column or Row		Format, Row or Column, Unhide	
Zoom	100% ▾	View, Zoom	

PROCEDURES CHECK

Matching: Identify the commands represented by the following buttons:

1. _____

2. _____

3. _____

4. _____

5. _____

6. _____

7. _____

8. _____

9. _____

10. _____

Completion: In the space provided at the right, indicate the correct term or command.

1. Make a cell active in this row to insert a new row between rows 11 and 12.   _____

2. Make a cell active in this column to insert a new column between E and F.   _____

3. Make a cell active here to freeze rows 1 through 9 and columns A and B.   _____

4. Do this action with the mouse on a column boundary to adjust the width to the length of the longest entry.   _____

5. Use this feature to automatically change all occurrences of a label, value, or format to another label, value, or format.   _____

6. List the steps you would complete to move the range A12:B14 to C16:D18 using the drag and drop method.

_____

_____

_____

7. List the steps you would complete to copy the range A5:A9 to A12:A16 using the menus.

_____

_____

_____

SKILLS REVIEW

Activity 1: EDITING, CLEARING, AND INSERTING CELLS; PERFORMING A SPELL CHECK

1. Open WB Invoice.
2. Save the workbook with Save <u>A</u>s and name it Excel S2-R1.
3. Change the cost in I20 from *4.58* to *4.97*.
4. Clear the contents of I16:I17.
5. Change the label in A21 from *Soup* to *Seafood Chowder Soup*.
6. Insert cells above E10:F10 and then key the following data in the new cells:
   E10 = **PO No.**
   F10 = **T6-1295**
7. Clear the contents of A8.
8. Complete a spelling check of the worksheet. (All names are spelled correctly.)
9. Save Excel S2-R1.

Activity 2: MOVING, COPYING, AND DELETING CELLS; INSERTING AND DELETING ROWS

1. With Excel S2-R1 open, move D3 to A8.
2. Move E11:F11 to E14:F14.
3. Copy A27 to A33.
4. Make cell F19 active, display the Delete dialog box, click Shift cells <u>u</u>p, and then click OK.
5. Delete the entire row for those rows that contain the labels *Milk*, *Assorted Juice*, and *Doughnuts*.
6. Insert a new row between *Prime Rib* and *Mixed Vegetables* and then key **Seafood Pasta** in column A of the new row.
7. Save Excel S2-R1.

Activity 3: ADJUSTING COLUMN WIDTH; REPLACING DATA; FORMATTING NUMBERS; INDENTING TEXT

1 With Excel S2-R1 open, select columns C and D and then adjust the width to the length of the longest entry (AutoFit).
2 Change the width of column E to 7.00 (54 pixels).
3 Select columns I through K and then adjust the width to the length of the longest entry (AutoFit).
4 Use the Replace feature to replace the value *33* with *37*.
5 Format F20 and F35 to Accounting.
6 Format F30 and F33 to Comma Style.
7 Format K20 and K30 to Percent Style with one decimal place.
8 Indent once A21:A29 and A31:A32.
9 Save Excel S2-R1.

Activity 4: CHANGING FONT, FONT ATTRIBUTES, AND ALIGNMENT; ADDING BORDERS AND SHADING; HIDING COLUMNS

1 With Excel S2-R1 open, change the font in A8 to 20-point Book Antiqua Bold. *(If Book Antiqua is not available on your computer system, substitute another font such as Times New Roman.)*
2 Merge and center A8 across columns A through F.
3 Change the font color in A8 to Red.
4 Change the fill color in A8 to Yellow.
5 Center the values in columns C and D and in F19.
6 Add a top and bottom border to A19:F19.
7 Add a bottom double border to F35.
8 Bold A19:F19 and F35.
9 Hide columns I through K.
10 Save Excel S2-R1.
11 Print and then close Excel S2-R1.

PERFORMANCE PLUS

Activity 1: FREEZING PANES AND CHANGING ZOOM, COLUMN WIDTH, FONT COLOR, AND FILL COLOR

1 Dana Hirsch, manager of The Waterfront Bistro, has asked you to review the *Inventory Units Purchased* report and modify it to make it more readable and to view as much data as possible in one window.
2 Open WB Inventory.
3 Save the workbook with Save <u>A</u>s and name it Excel S2-P1.
4 Make the following changes:
   a Freeze panes so you can scroll the worksheet without losing the column and row headings.
   b Change the zoom so you can view as much of the worksheet as possible to minimize scrolling. Make sure the cells are still readable. *(Note: Depending on your monitor size, change the <u>C</u>ustom setting to a value between 50% and 80%.)*

    c Adjust all column widths to the length of the longest entry (AutoFit).

    d Change the color of the shading behind the title *Inventory Units Purchased*. You determine the color.

    e Change the font color and the shading color for A2:O2. You determine the colors.

5 Change the page orientation to landscape. *(Hint: Do this at the Page Setup dialog box with the Page tab selected.)*

6 Save Excel S2-P1.

7 Print page 1 only and then close Excel S2-P1.

Activity 2: EDITING CELLS; INSERTING AND HIDING COLUMNS; COPYING A FORMULA; FORMATTING A WORKSHEET

1 Bobbie Sinclair of Performance Threads has started preparing a workbook that tracks the costs of costume research, design, and production for the Marquee Productions project. You have been asked to complete the workbook.

2 Open PT Costumes.

3 Save the workbook with Save <u>A</u>s and name it Excel S2-P2.

4 Complete the worksheet using the following information:

    a Design costs should be *28.50* instead of *21.50*.

    b Insert a new column between *Fabric* and *Total Cost* and key the column heading **Notions** in J9. Key the values in J10:J14 as follows:

Val Wingfield	**110.00**
Eunice Billings	**78.43**
Tony Salvatore	**93.67**
Celia Gopf	**143.66**
Jade Norwich	**169.42**

    c The formula to calculate total cost for each costume is incorrect. Enter the correct formula for the first costume (K10) and then copy the formula to K11:K14. *(Hint: The current formula does not include the Fabric and Notions costs.)*

    d Format the numeric cells in an appropriate style.

    e Change the alignment of any headings that could be improved in appearance.

    f Merge and center the titles in A6 and A7 over the columns.

    g Apply font and color changes to enhance the appearance of the worksheet.

    h Hide the *Costume Fee* and *Profit* columns.

5 Print the worksheet in landscape orientation.

6 Save Excel S2-P2.

7 Close Excel S2-P2.

Activity 3: COMPLETING AND FORMATTING A WORKSHEET

1 Camille Matsui, production assistant for Marquee Productions, has requested that Performance Threads send an invoice for the five custom-made costumes separate from the costume rentals. Bobbie Sinclair has started the invoice and has asked you to finish it.

2 Open PT Invoice.

3 Save the workbook with Save <u>A</u>s and name it Excel S2-P3.

4 Complete the invoice using the following information:

    a Key the current date in G6.

    b Each custom costume fee is $2,500.00. Enter this value in F15:F19.

   c Total the costume fees in F20.

   d A transportation and storage container for each of the five costumes is $75.00. Enter the appropriate formula in G22 that will calculate the fee for five containers.

   e Enter in F23 the delivery for all five costumes as $112.50.

   f Enter the formula in F24 that will add the total for the costume fees with the additional charges.

   g Enter the formula in F25 that will calculate 7% GST (Goods and Services Tax) on the total including additional charges.

   h Enter the formula to total the invoice in F26 as the sum of F24 and F25.

5 Format the worksheet to improve the appearance of the invoice.

6 Save Excel S2-P3.

7 Print and then close Excel S2-P3.

Activity 4: PERFORMING SPELL CHECK; ADJUSTING COLUMN WIDTH; EDITING CELLS; USING FIND AND REPLACE; HIDING COLUMNS; FORMATTING WORKSHEETS

1 Sam Vestering, manager of North American Distribution for Worldwide Enterprises, has created a workbook to summarize revenues from distribution of Marquee Productions' film *Two By Two*. You have been asked to review the worksheet and make corrections and enhancements to the appearance.

2 Open WE Revenue.

3 Save the workbook with Save <u>A</u>s and name it Excel S2-P4.

4 Make the following corrections:

   a Perform a spelling check.

   b Adjust column widths so all data is completely visible.

   c Check the Projected Box Office Sales with the data in Excel S1-P3 and change any values that do not match. *(Note: You can check these values on page 32 if you did not complete Performance Plus Activity 3.)*

   d Enter the formulas to calculate the Box Office Variance as Box Office Sales minus Projected Box Office Sales.

   e Change all of the theaters named *Cinema House* to *Cinema Magic*.

   f Apply formatting enhancements to improve the appearance of the worksheet.

5 Print Excel S2-P4.

6 Hide columns H and I.

7 Print Excel S2-P4.

8 Save and then close Excel S2-P4.

Activity 5: FINDING THE SELECT ALL BUTTON

1 Use Excel's Help feature to find out where the Select All button is located in the Excel window.

2 Open Excel S2-P1.

3 Save the workbook with Save <u>A</u>s and name it Excel S2-P5.

4 Click the Select All button.

5 Click the Align Right and Italic buttons on the Formatting toolbar.

6 Scroll the worksheet to view the new formats.

7 Change columns A and B to Align Left.

8 Save Excel S2-P5.

9 Print page 1 only and then close Excel S2-P5.

Activity 6: FINDING INFORMATION ON DATES

1 Use Excel's Help feature to find information on how Excel stores dates and how they can be used in a formula.
2 Open Excel S2-P3.
3 Save the workbook with Save As and name it Excel S2-P6.
4 Add the label *Due Date:* to F12.
5 Create a formula in G12 that will add 30 days to the date of the invoice.
6 Save and print Excel S2-P6.
7 Change the date of the invoice to *May 10, 2003*.
8 Print and then close Excel S2-P6 without saving the changes.

Activity 7: FINDING INFORMATION ON SPLITTING CELLS

1 Use Excel's Help feature to find information on how to split cells that have been merged and centered.
2 Open Excel S2-R1.
3 Save the workbook with Save As and name it Excel S2-P7.
4 Split the merged cells A8:F8 containing the label *Invoice*.
5 Preview and then print Excel S2-P7.
6 Save and then close Excel S2-P7.

Activity 8: LOCATING INFORMATION ON THEATER ARTS PROGRAMS

1 You are considering enrolling in a Drama/Theater Arts program at a college or university. Search the Internet for available programs in post-secondary schools in the United States and Canada. Choose five schools that interest you the most and find out as much as you can about the costs of attending these schools. Try to find information on costs beyond tuition and books, such as transportation and room and board.
2 Create a workbook that will summarize the information on the schools you have selected.
3 Apply formatting enhancements to the worksheet.
4 Save the workbook and name it Excel S2-P8.
5 Print and then close Excel S2-P8.

EXCEL

Using Functions, Setting Print Options, and Adding Visual Elements

Functions in Excel are grouped into categories such as Statistical, Date, Financial, and Logical. The Insert Function dialog box can be used to find a preprogrammed function by searching based on a description or by browsing a list of functions within a category. The Page Setup dialog box is used to change options for printing worksheets such as changing margins, centering on a page, and repeating column or row labels on multiple sheets. Adding visual elements such as charts or drawn objects to a worksheet can assist the reader with interpreting numerical data. For example, a chart can illustrate variances in sales more dramatically than the numbers alone. Objects such as text boxes can be drawn to guide a reader's attention to a cell or range of cells. In this section you will learn the skills and complete the projects described here.

Note: Before beginning this section, delete the Excel S2 *folder on your disk. Next, copy to your disk the* Excel S3 *subfolder from the* Excel *folder on the CD that accompanies this textbook, and then make* Excel S3 *the active folder.*

Skills

- Use the AVERAGE, MAX, and MIN formulas to perform statistical analysis
- Create NOW and DATE formulas
- Determine loan payment amounts using the PMT function
- Create an IF formula to return a result based on a logical test
- Change margins
- Center a worksheet horizontally and vertically
- Insert headers and footers
- Print row headings, column headings, and gridlines
- Scale a worksheet to fit within a specified number of pages
- Create, edit, and format charts
- Insert, size, and move a picture
- Draw arrows and text boxes

Projects

Add function formulas and set print options for the *Inventory Units Purchased* and *Quarterly Expenses* reports; enter Date functions in an invoice and change the print options; calculate loan payment amounts for an expansion project; use an IF function to calculate bonuses and change print options; create and modify charts; insert pictures; and draw an arrow and text box in an *Operating Expenses and Cost of Sales* worksheet.

Set print options for the *Theatre Arts Co-Op Work Term Placements* report; add a formula based on a date and create and format charts for a grades analysis report.

Calculate commissions and analyze data in a *Sales Agent Commission* report; insert a picture and apply formatting enhancements to a *European Destinations* report.

Calculate payments for a loan to construct a new building.

3.1 Using Statistical Functions AVERAGE, MAX, and MIN

You learned about functions when you used the AutoSum button, which assisted with entering the SUM function. Excel includes numerous built-in formulas that are grouped into function categories. The Statistical category contains several functions that can be used to perform statistical analysis on data, such as calculating medians, variances, frequencies, and so on. The structure of a function formula begins with the equals sign (=), followed by the name of the function, and then the *argument* within parentheses. The argument is the term given to the values to be included in the calculation. The structure of the argument is dependent on the function being used and can include a single range of cells, multiple ranges, single cell references, or a combination thereof.

PROJECT: You decide to include some basic statistical analysis in the *Inventory Units Purchased* report for The Waterfront Bistro such as the average quantity purchased, the maximum units purchased, and the minimum units purchased.

STEPS

1 Open WB Inventory.

2 Save the workbook with Save As and name it Excel S3-01.

3 Make C3 the active cell and then freeze the panes.

4 Enter the following labels in the cells indicated:

A58 = **Average Units Purchased**
A59 = **Maximum Units Purchased**
A60 = **Minimum Units Purchased**

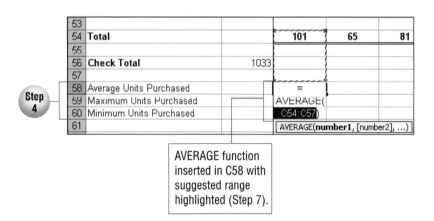

Step 4

AVERAGE function inserted in C58 with suggested range highlighted (Step 7).

5 Make C58 the active cell.

In the next steps you will insert the AVERAGE function to determine the arithmetic mean of the cells in column C. If an empty cell or a cell containing text is included in the argument, Excel ignores the cell when determining the result. If, however, the cell contains a zero value, it is included in the average calculation.

6 Click the down-pointing triangle to the right of the AutoSum button on the Standard toolbar.

7 Click Average in the drop-down list.

Excel inserts the formula =AVERAGE(C54:C57) in the active cell with the suggested range highlighted. In the next step you will drag to select the correct range and then complete the formula.

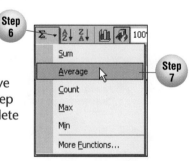

Step 6

Step 7

(8) Scroll up the worksheet until you can see C3. Position the cell pointer over C3, hold down the left mouse button, drag down to C52, and then release the left mouse button.

> Excel inserts the range *C3:C52* in the formula and the moving marquee expands to display the selected cells. Notice that Excel color codes the range entry in the formula with the expanded range border.

(9) Press Enter or click the Enter button on the Formula bar.

> Excel returns the result *2.02* in C58.

(10) Make C59 the active cell.

(11) Click the down-pointing triangle to the right of the AutoSum button on the Standard toolbar and then click Max in the drop-down list.

> The MAX function returns the largest value in the argument.

(12) Key **C3:C52** and then press Enter.

> Excel returns the result *6* in C59. Keying the range into the formula is sometimes faster if you are sure of the starting and ending cell references.

Step 12

58	Average Units Purchased		2.02
59	Maximum Units Purchased		=MAX(C3:
60	Minimum Units Purchased		C52)
61			MAX(**number1**, [number2], ...)

(13) With C60 the active cell, key the function **=MIN(C3:C52)** and then press Enter.

> The MIN function returns the smallest value in the argument. You can key the entire function directly into the cell if you know the name of the function you want to use and the structure of the argument.

PROBLEM Cell displays *#NAME?* A keying error in the formula causes this indicator to appear and a Trace Error button will appear when the cell is activated. Click the Trace Error button [⟐] to access error checking tools.

54	Total		101	65
55				
56	**Check Total**	1033		
57				
58	Average Units Purchased		2	
59	Maximum Units Purchased		6	
60	Minimum Units Purchased		0	
61				

Drag the fill handle right to column N.

Step 15

(14) Format C58:C60 to the Number format with zero decimal places.

(15) Select C58:C60 and then drag the fill handle right to column N.

> This copies the AVERAGE, MAX, and MIN formulas to columns D through N.

PROBLEM Scrolling too fast? Don't let go of the mouse—drag it in the opposite direction.

(16) Click in any cell to deselect C58:N60.

(17) Save and then close Excel S3-01.

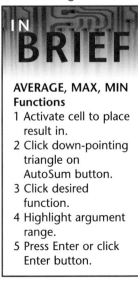

IN **BRIEF**

AVERAGE, MAX, MIN Functions
1 Activate cell to place result in.
2 Click down-pointing triangle on AutoSum button.
3 Click desired function.
4 Highlight argument range.
5 Press Enter or click Enter button.

3.2 Using Date Functions NOW and DATE

Excel stores dates as a serial number calculated from January 1, 1900, as serial number 1 and increased sequentially. Times are stored as decimal fractions representing portions of a day. This enables calculations to be performed on cells containing dates and times. The Date & Time category in the Insert Function dialog box contains functions that can be used to write formulas for cells containing dates. Cells containing dates and times can be formatted using the Format Cells dialog box to display the date or time in various formats.

PROJECT: You will open an invoice to Performance Threads and use the NOW function to enter the current date, and then calculate the due date by entering a formula to add 30 days to the invoice date. The DATE function will be used to enter the date The Waterfront Bistro opened.

STEPS

1. Open WB Invoice2.

2. Save the workbook with Save As and name it Excel S3-02.

3. Make E7 the active cell, key **=NOW()**, and then press Enter.

    Excel inserts the current date and time in E7 and the column width automatically expands to accommodate the length of the entry.

4. Make E9 the active cell and then key the formula **=E7+30** to calculate the due date as 30 days from the invoice date.

5. Make E5 the active cell and then click the down-pointing triangle to the right of the AutoSum button on the Standard toolbar.

6. Click More Functions in the drop-down list.

    The Insert Function dialog box opens. In this dialog box you can search for a function by keying a phrase describing the type of formula you want in the Search for a function text box and then clicking the Go button, or by selecting a category name and then browsing a list of functions.

7. At the Insert Function dialog box, click the down-pointing triangle to the right of the Or select a category option box and then click *Date & Time* in the drop-down list.

    The Select a function list box displays an alphabetical list of date and time functions. Clicking a function name in the Select a function list box causes the formula with its argument structure and a description to appear below the list box. For more information on the selected function name, click the *Help on this function* hyperlink at the bottom left of the Insert Function dialog box to open the Microsoft Help window.

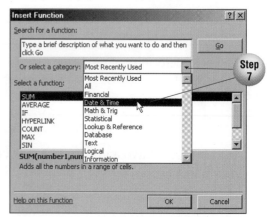

8. With the function name *DATE* already selected in the Select a function list box, read the description of the formula and then click OK.

    The Function Arguments dialog box opens with a text box for each section of the function argument.

(9) Key **1977** in the Year text box.

(10) Press Tab to move the insertion point to the Month text box and then key **06**.

(11) Press Tab to move the insertion point to the Day text box and then key **15**.

(12) Click OK to close the Function Arguments dialog box.

> The Function Arguments dialog box displayed the serial number for June 15, 1977, as *28291*; however, cell E5 displays the date. Notice the formula in the Formula bar is *=DATE(1977,6,15)*.

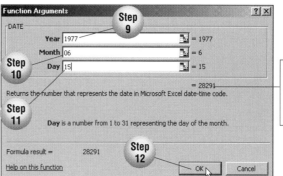

This is the serial number representing June 15, 1977.

(13) With E5 the active cell, click Format and then Cells.

(14) If necessary, click the Number tab in the Format Cells dialog box.

> Since the active cell contained a date function, the Date category will be automatically selected in the Format Cells dialog box with the Number tab selected.

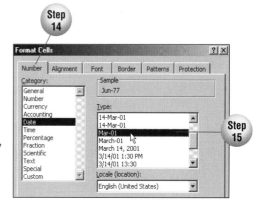

(15) Scroll the list of formats in the Type list box, click the format that will display the date as *mmm-yy (Mar-01)*, and then click OK.

(16) Format E5 to 9-point Arial Italic.

(17) Select E7:E9 and then display the Format Cells dialog box with the Number tab selected.

(18) Click *Date* in the Category list box. Scroll down the Type list box, click the format that will display the date as *dd-mmm-yyyy (14-Mar-2001)*, and then click OK.

(19) Drag the right column boundary line for column E to the left until the yellow box displays *Width: 10.00 (75 pixels)*.

(20) Save and then close Excel S3-02.

In Addition

TIME Function

Time values are stored as decimal numbers that represent the portion of a day starting at 0 (12:00:00 AM), and continuing up to 0.99999999, representing (23:59:59 PM). The format of the TIME function is *=TIME(hour,minute,second)*. In the time worksheet shown at the right, the formula *=(C2-B2)*24* is used to calculate how many hours the employees worked.

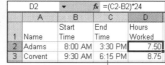

The entry stored in C3 is *=TIME(18,15,0)*.

IN BRIEF

Date Function
1. Make desired cell active.
2. Click down-pointing triangle on AutoSum button.
3. Click More Functions.
4. Click down-pointing triangle next to Or select a category.
5. Click *Date & Time* in the drop-down list.
6. Click desired function name in Select a function list box.
7. Click OK.
8. Enter argument criteria in the Function Arguments dialog box.
9. Click OK.

3.3 Using Financial Function PMT

Excel's financial functions can be used to calculate depreciation, interest rates, payments, terms, present values, future values, and so on. The PMT function is used to calculate a payment for a loan based on constant payments, a constant interest rate, and a set period of time.

PROJECT: The Waterfront Bistro is planning a major expansion next year. the manager, Dana Hirsch, has asked you to calculate monthly payments for two construction loan scenarios.

STEPS

1. Open WB Financials.

2. Save the workbook with Save As and name it Excel S3-03.

3. Make B12 the active cell.

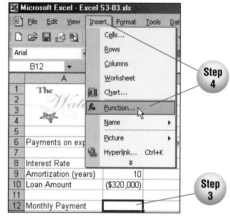

PROBLEM?

Cell B12 is not empty? Check that A12 contains the text *Monthly Payment*. If it does not, click the sheet tab named *Construction Loan* at the bottom of the worksheet area just above the Status bar.

4. Click Insert and then Function.

   Clicking Insert and then Function is another method used to display the Insert Function dialog box. Notice that Date & Time (the most recently displayed list of functions) is the category currently shown. In the next steps you will use the Search for a function feature to find the PMT function.

5. With the entry *Type a brief description of what you want to do and then click Go* already selected in the Search for a function text box, key **Loan Payments**, and then click the Go button.

   Two functions display in the Select a function list box and the category name changes to *Recommended*.

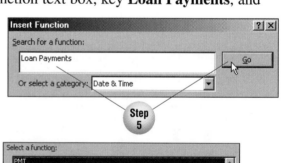

6. With PMT already selected in the Select a function list box, click OK.

7. Drag the Function Arguments dialog box to the right of column B.

8. With the insertion point positioned in the Rate text box, click the mouse in B8 and then key **/12**.

   Since the interest rate is stated per annum, keying */12* divides the annual interest rate by 12 to obtain a monthly interest rate.

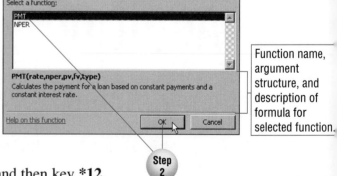

Function name, argument structure, and description of formula for selected function.

9. Click in the Nper text box, click B9, and then key ***12**.

   The loan period, or *amortization*, is stated in years. Keying *12* multiplies the number of years times 12 to calculate the number of monthly payments that will be made on the loan.

10 Click in the Pv text box and then click B10.

> Pv is the *Present value*, or the principal amount that is being borrowed.

11 Click OK.

> Excel returns the payment amount *$4,301.81* in B12.

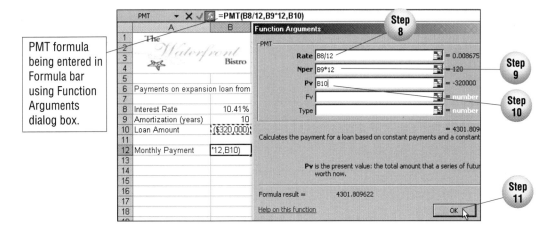

PMT formula being entered in Formula bar using Function Arguments dialog box.

12 Save Excel S3-03.

> In the next steps you will modify the amortization period and the interest rate to see the effect on the monthly payment amount.

13 Make B8 the active cell and edit the interest rate amount from *10.41%* to *11.25%*.

14 Make B9 the active cell and edit the amortization period from *10* years to *8* years.

> Excel recalculates the monthly payment with the new interest rate and term to *$5,069.95*.

15 Save Excel S3-03.

In Addition

FV Function

The FV function is used to return the future value of an investment based on periodic, constant payments and a constant interest rate. The FV function is entered as *=FV(Rate,Nper,Pmt)* where rate is the interest rate per period, Nper is the total number of payments that will be made into the investment, and Pmt is the amount invested each period. FV assumes the payment amount will not change over the life of the investment.

Example: Assume a constant payment each year for 10 years of $5,000 into a retirement account that earns 7.75% interest per year. The formula *=FV(7.75%,10,-5000)* would return the result $71,578.53.

IN BRIEF

Financial Functions
1. Make desired cell active.
2. Click Insert, Function.
3. Click down-pointing triangle next to Or select a category.
4. Click *Financial* in the drop-down list.
5. Click desired function name in Select a function list box.
6. Click OK.
7. Enter argument criteria in the Function Arguments dialog box.
8. Click OK.

3.4 Using Logical Function IF

The IF function returns one of two values in a cell based on a true or false answer to a question called a *logical test*. For example, if the logical test is true, value *x* is placed in the cell. If the logical test is false, value *y* is placed in the cell. The format of an IF function is *=IF(logical_test,value_if_true,value_if_false)*. Logical functions allow you to use Excel to insert text or values based on a set of circumstances that you define. For example, a teacher could create an IF statement to insert the word *Pass* in a cell if a

student's mark is greater than or equal to 50%, or the word *Fail* if the mark is less than 50%.

PROJECT: The dining room staff at The Waterfront Bistro receives a year-end bonus if profit targets are met. The bonus amount is 0.75% of actual profit if years of service are greater than or equal to 4 years, and 0.45% for years of service less than 4 years. You will create the formula in the *Bonus* worksheet to calculate these bonuses.

STEPS

1. With Excel S3-03 open, click the sheet tab labeled *Bonus* located at the bottom of the screen just above the Status bar.

2. Make C7 in the *Bonus* worksheet the active cell.

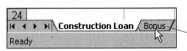
Step 1

3. Key **=IF(B7>=4,$F$7*$H$7,$F$7*$I$7)** and then press Enter.

   Excel returns the value *1073.693* in C7. The IF function entered in C7 is explained in Figure E3.1. The cell references in the true and false arguments contain dollar symbols to make them *absolute references*. Notice a dollar symbol is keyed before both the column letter and the row number in the absolute cell references. The dollar symbol instructs Excel not to change the column or row relative to the destination when the formula is copied. Since the formula will be copied to rows 8–12, absolute references are required within the source formula for those cells that contain the percentages.

FIGURE E3.1
The IF Function

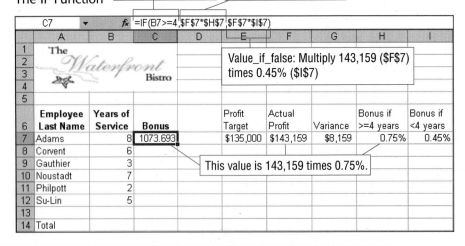

If you make a keying error, Excel displays a message and highlights the approximate area within the formula where the error occurred.

PROBLEM**?**

④ Press the up arrow to move the active cell back to C7.

⑤ Drag the fill handle down to row 12.

⑥ With C7:C12 still selected, click the Currency Style button on the Formatting toolbar.

⑦ Make C14 the active cell and then use AutoSum to calculate the total.

⑧ Save Excel S3-03.

⑨ Close Excel S3-03.

	A	B	C	D	E	F	G	H	I
1	The								
2		Waterfront							
3			Bistro						
4									
5									
6	Employee Last Name	Years of Service	Bonus		Profit Target	Actual Profit	Variance	Bonus if >=4 years	Bonus if <4 years
7	Adams	8	$1,073.69		$135,000	$143,159	$8,159	0.75%	0.45%
8	Corvent	6	$1,073.69						
9	Gauthier	3	$ 644.22						
10	Noustadt	7	$1,073.69						
11	Philpott	2	$ 644.22						
12	Su-Lin	5	$1,073.69						
13									
14	Total		$5,583.20						

Steps 5–6

Step 7

In Addition

Nested IF Function

If more than two actions are required when a logical test is performed, a nested IF function is used. For example, if three bonus rates were dependent on years of service for the dining room staff, the IF function entered in C7 would not have been sufficient. Assume the dining room staff receives 0.75% if they have 4 years of service or more, 0.45% for 2–4 years, and 0.1% for less than 2 years. The IF function required to calculate the bonus would be:

=IF(B7>=4,$F$7*0.75%,IF(B7>=2,$F$7*0.45%,$F$7*0.1%))

The two parentheses at the end of the argument are required to close both IF statements.

IN BRIEF

IF Function
1. Make desired cell active.
2. Click Insert, Function.
3. Click down-pointing triangle next to Or select a category.
4. Click Logical in the drop-down list.
5. Click IF in the Select a function list box.
6. Click OK.
7. Enter test condition in Logical_test text box.
8. Enter action required in Value_if_true text box.
9. Enter action required in Value_if_false text box.
10. Click OK.

3.5 Changing Margins; Centering a Worksheet on the Page

The margin on an Excel worksheet is the blank space at the top, bottom, left, and right edges of the page and the beginning of the printed text. Margin settings can be changed in the Page Setup dialog box or by dragging the margin handles on the Print Preview screen. The bottom section of the Margins tab in the Page Setup dialog box contains check boxes to center the worksheet on the page horizontally and/or vertically.

PROJECT: You will preview the Invoice to Performance Threads, adjust the left margin to balance the worksheet on the page and then print. You will center the *Bonus* worksheet horizontally and vertically and print it in landscape orientation.

S T E P S

① Open Excel S3-02.

② Click the Print Preview button 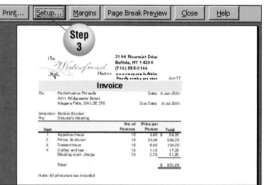 on the Standard toolbar.

> Notice the Invoice is unbalanced at the left edge of the page with a larger amount of white space on the right side. One method of correcting this is to change the left margin.

③ Click the Setup button on the Print Preview toolbar.

④ Click the Margins tab in the Page Setup dialog box.

⑤ Click the up-pointing triangle to the right of the Left spin box until *1.75* displays, and then click OK.

> Alternatively, you can drag the number in the Left spin box to select the current value and then key the new margin setting.The worksheet now appears balanced between the left and right edges of the page.

⑥ Click the Print button on the Print Preview toolbar.

> The Print Preview window closes and the Print dialog box appears.

⑦ At the Print dialog box, click OK.

⑧ Save and then close Excel S3-02.

⑨ Open Excel S3-03 and make sure the *Bonus* worksheet is the active worksheet. *(Hint: Click the Bonus worksheet tab at the bottom of the worksheet area if it is not currently displayed.)*

⑩ Click File and then Page Setup.

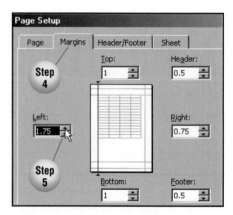

(11) Click the Page tab in the Page Setup dialog box.

(12) Click Landscape.

(13) Click the Margins tab.

(14) Click the Horizontally and Vertically check boxes in the Center on page section, and then click OK.

(15) Click the Print Preview button on the Standard toolbar.

> The worksheet is displayed centered both horizontally and vertically on the page.

(16) Close the Print Preview window.

(17) Click the Print button on the Standard toolbar.

(18) Save Excel S3-03.

Step 11

Step 12

Step 14

In Addition

Changing Margins in Print Preview

Click the Margins button on the Print Preview toolbar to display column handles and horizontal and vertical guidelines. Drag the horizontal or vertical guidelines to adjust the left, right, top, bottom, and header and footer margins. Drag the column handles to adjust the column widths. Click Margins again to turn off the display of column handles and guidelines.

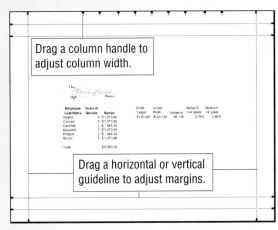

Drag a column handle to adjust column width.

Drag a horizontal or vertical guideline to adjust margins.

In Brief

Changing Margins
1 Click File, Page Setup.
2 Click Margins tab.
3 Change required margin setting.
4 Click OK.

Centering Worksheet
1 Click File, Page Setup.
2 Click Margins tab.
3 Click Horizontally and/or Vertically check box.
4 Click OK.

3.6 Inserting Headers and Footers

A header is text that prints at the top of each worksheet and a footer is text that prints at the bottom of each worksheet. Headers and footers are created in the Page Setup dialog box. Excel includes predefined headers and footers that can be selected from a drop-down list, or you can create your own custom header or footer text. Header and footer text does not appear in the worksheet area—it is a function that affects printing.

PROJECT: To distinguish the *Bonus* worksheet, you will create a custom header that prints the current date aligned at the right margin and a custom footer that prints your name aligned at the left margin and the file name aligned at the right margin.

S T E P S

1. With Excel S3-03 open, click File and then Page Setup.

2. Click the Header/Footer tab in the Page Setup dialog box.

3. Click the Custom Header button.

   This displays the Header window as shown in Figure E3.2.

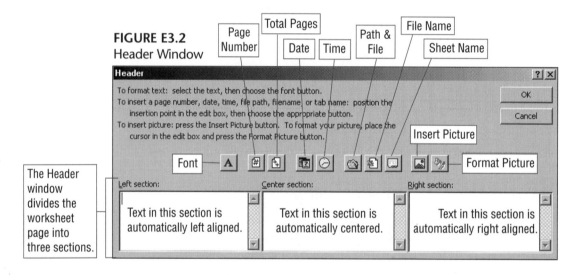

FIGURE E3.2
Header Window

The Header window divides the worksheet page into three sections.

4. At the Header window, press Tab twice to move the insertion point to the Right section text box, or click the I-beam pointer in the Right section.

5. Key **Date Printed:**, press the spacebar once, and then click the Date button in the Header window.

   Excel inserts the code *&[Date]*, which will cause the current date to be inserted at the location of the code when the worksheet is printed.

6. Click OK to close the Header window.

   The custom header now appears in the preview section of the Header/Footer tab in the Page Setup dialog box.

7 Click Custom Footer.

The Footer window contains the same elements as the Header window.

8 At the Footer window, key your first and last name in the Left section.

9 Press Tab twice to move the insertion point to the Right section text box, or click the I-beam pointer in the Right section.

10 Click the File Name button  in the Footer window.

Excel inserts the code *&[File]* which will cause the workbook file name to be printed.

11 Click OK to close the Footer window.

The custom header and custom footer display in the preview sections of the Page Setup dialog box with the Header/Footer tab selected, as shown in Figure E3.

12 Click OK to close the Page Setup dialog box.

13 Display the *Bonus* worksheet in Print Preview.

14 Print the *Bonus* worksheet.

15 Save and then close Excel S3-03.

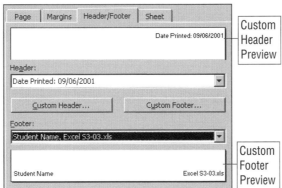

FIGURE E3.3 Header/Footer Previews in Page Setup Dialog Box

In *Addition*

Header and Footer Margins

By default, a header will print 0.5 inch from the top of the page and the footer will print 0.5 inch from the bottom of the page. Display the Page Setup dialog box and select the Margins tab to alter these settings.

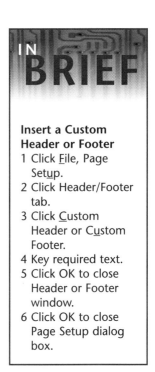

IN BRIEF

Insert a Custom Header or Footer

1 Click File, Page Setup.
2 Click Header/Footer tab.
3 Click Custom Header or Custom Footer.
4 Key required text.
5 Click OK to close Header or Footer window.
6 Click OK to close Page Setup dialog box.

3.7 Printing Headings and Gridlines; Scaling a Worksheet

Column and row headings can be printed at the top and left edges of multiple pages when a large worksheet prints on more than one page. Turning on the gridlines will cause Excel to print the horizontal and vertical row and column boundary lines. A large worksheet can be reduced in size proportionately to fit within a specified number of pages.

PROJECT: Dana Hirsch has asked you to print the *Inventory Units Purchased* report. You will open the workbook and print two versions of the report—one at full size that includes headings and gridlines, and another that reduces the report to fit within one page.

STEPS

1. Open Excel S3-01.

2. Click File and then Page Setup.

3. Click the Page tab in the Page Setup dialog box, click Landscape, and then click OK.

4. Display the worksheet in Print Preview, and view all of the pages in the Print Preview window. *(Hint: Click the Next and Previous buttons on the Print Preview toolbar to view all of the pages.)*

5. Close Print Preview.

6. Click File, Page Setup, and then click the Sheet tab.

    The Print titles section in the Sheet tab contains two options: Rows to repeat at top and Columns to repeat at left. Use these options to print row or column labels at the top and left edges of each page in the printed worksheet.

7. Click the Collapse Dialog button 🔲 to the right of the Rows to repeat at top text box.

    This reduces the size of the dialog box to the active option only. You can now enter the range by selecting cells within the worksheet.

8. Select rows 1 and 2.

9. Click the Collapse Dialog button to redisplay the entire Page Setup dialog box.

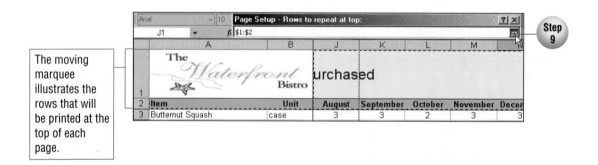

The moving marquee illustrates the rows that will be printed at the top of each page.

Step 9

10. Click in the Columns to repeat at left text box and then click the Collapse Dialog button.

(11) Select columns A and B and then click the Collapse Dialog button.

PROBLEM **?**

If necessary, drag the Title bar of the collapsed dialog box to move it out of the way so you can select columns A and B.

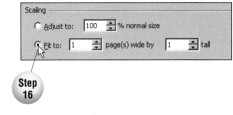

Steps 10–11

(12) Click the Gridlines check box in the Print section.

Step 12

(13) Click OK to close the Page Setup dialog box.

(14) Print Excel S3-01.

> Depending on your printer, this printout may take a few moments to print.

(15) Click File, Page Setup, and then click the Page tab.

(16) Click Fit to 1 page(s) wide by 1 tall in the Scaling section.

(17) Click the Margins tab, click the Horizontally and Vertically check boxes, and then click OK to close the Page Setup dialog box.

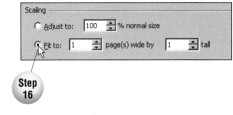

Step 16

PROBLEM **?**

If the printout is too small to read, change the percentage in the Adjust to spin box in the Page tab of the Page Setup dialog box.

(18) Save and then print Excel S3-01.

(19) Close Excel S3-01.

In Addition

Inserting and Removing a Page Break

To insert your own horizontal page break in a worksheet, select the row just below where you want the break to occur, click Insert, and then click Page Break. To insert a vertical page break, select the column just to the right of where you want the break to occur. The Page Break option on the Insert menu changes to Remove Page Break when a row or column is selected where a page break was inserted. Page breaks cannot be inserted in a worksheet if the scaling option is set to 1 page wide by 1 page tall in the Page Setup dialog box.

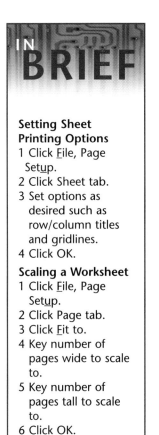

IN BRIEF

Setting Sheet Printing Options
1 Click File, Page Setup.
2 Click Sheet tab.
3 Set options as desired such as row/column titles and gridlines.
4 Click OK.

Scaling a Worksheet
1 Click File, Page Setup.
2 Click Page tab.
3 Click Fit to.
4 Key number of pages wide to scale to.
5 Key number of pages tall to scale to.
6 Click OK.

3.8 Creating a Chart

Data in a worksheet can be presented visually by creating a chart. A chart is sometimes referred to as a *graph*. The chart can be placed in the same worksheet as the data or it can be inserted into its own sheet. The Chart Wizard automates the process of creating charts through a series of four dialog boxes that are used to select the chart type, define the source data, select chart options, and specify the chart location.

PROJECT: Operating expenses by quarter for The Waterfront Bistro are stored in a workbook named WB Expenses. Dana Hirsch has requested that you create a chart to compare the expenses in each quarter and another chart to show each expense as a proportion of the total expenses.

S T E P S

1. Open WB Expenses.

2. Save the workbook with Save As and name it Excel S3-04.

3. Select A3:E9.

    The first step in creating a chart is to select the range of cells containing the data you want to chart.

4. Click the Chart Wizard button 📊 on the Standard toolbar.

5. The default choice in the <u>C</u>hart type list box is *Column*. Click the first chart in the second row of the Chart sub-<u>t</u>ype section (Clustered column with a 3-D visual effect) and then click <u>N</u>ext.

    The first Chart Wizard dialog box is used to select a chart type and subtype.

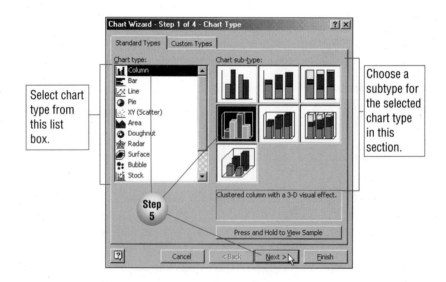

Select chart type from this list box.

Choose a subtype for the selected chart type in this section.

6 Make sure the Data range displays as *=Sheet1!$A$3:$E$9* and then click Next.

> The second Chart Wizard dialog box is used to define the source data that will be included to generate the chart.

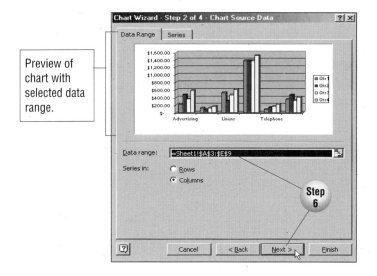

PROBLEM? If the displayed range is incorrect, click the Collapse Dialog button, select the correct range, and then click the Collapse Dialog button again.

Use these tabs to add and/or format chart options.

7 With the Titles tab selected in the Chart Options dialog box, click in the Chart title text box, key **Operating Expenses**, and then click Next.

> The third Chart Wizard dialog box is where chart options can be added to enhance the chart readability and appearance.

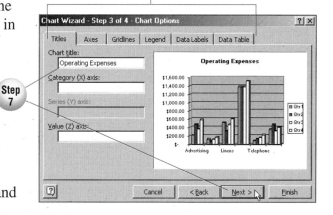

8 Click the As new sheet option and then click Finish.

> At the fourth Chart Wizard dialog box, the chart can be inserted in its own sheet or as an object in the active worksheet. Charts inserted in their own sheet are initially labeled *Chart1* and are automatically scaled to fill the entire page.

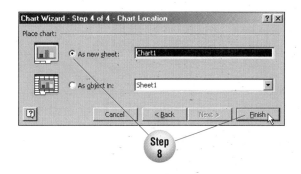

(continued)

⑨ Click the Print Preview button to view how the chart will print.

⑩ Click the Close button on the Print Preview toolbar.

⑪ Click the *Sheet1* worksheet tab at the bottom of the chart window to return to the *Operating Expenses* worksheet.

⑫ Click in any blank cell in the worksheet to deselect the range A3:E9.

⑬ Select the range A3:A9, hold down the Ctrl key, and then select the range F3:F9.

> Holding down the Ctrl key while dragging another group of cells allows you to select nonadjacent ranges.

⑭ Click the Chart Wizard button.

⑮ Click *Pie* in the Chart type list box, click the middle chart in the first row of the Chart sub-type section (Pie with a 3-D visual effect), and then click Next.

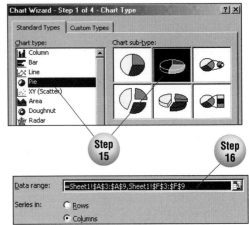

⑯ Make sure the Data range displays as =*Sheet1!$A$3:$A$9,Sheet1!$F$3:$F$9* and then click Next.

⑰ With the Titles tab selected, click in the Chart title text box after the word *Total*, press the spacebar, and then key **Operating Expenses**.

⑱ Click the Data Labels tab, click the Percentage check box in the Label Contains section, and then click Next.

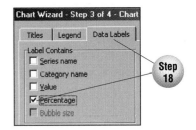

⑲ Click Finish at the last Chart Wizard dialog box.

> The chart is inserted as an object in the active worksheet and the Chart toolbar appears. Black sizing handles display around the perimeter of the chart. These handles indicate the chart is selected and can be moved or resized.

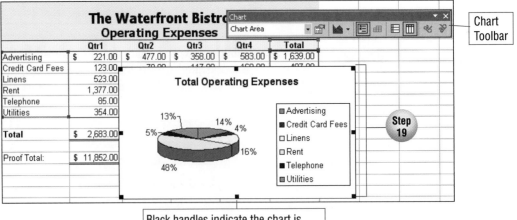

Black handles indicate the chart is selected and can be moved or resized.

20 Position the mouse pointer within a white area inside the chart, drag the mouse until the top left corner of the chart is positioned in A15, and then release the mouse button.

> The pointer changes to a four-headed arrow move icon as you drag the chart.

21 Position the mouse pointer on the black sizing handle at the bottom right corner of the chart until the pointer changes to a double-headed diagonal arrow. Drag the pointer down and right until the dashed border is positioned at the bottom right corner of F30 and then release the mouse button.

PROBLEM ?

> Having difficulty resizing the chart? First scroll down the window until you can see row 30.

22 Click in any cell within the worksheet to deselect the chart.

23 Click the Print Preview button to view the worksheet and the chart together on the same page.

24 Click the Setup button on the Print Preview toolbar.

25 At the Page Setup dialog box, click the Margins tab, center the worksheet and chart horizontally and vertically on the page, and then click OK.

26 Click the Print button.

27 At the Print dialog box, click Entire workbook in the Print what section, and then click OK.

28 Save Excel S3-04.

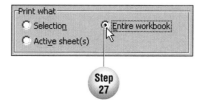

Step 27

In Addition

Printing Only the Chart

To print only the chart in a worksheet containing cells as well as a chart, click the chart to select it before clicking the Print button. The chart will automatically be scaled to fit the entire page.

IN BRIEF

Create a Chart
1 Select source cells.
2 Click Chart Wizard button.
3 Select chart type and subtype and click Next.
4 Verify data range/series and click Next.
5 Select chart options and click Next.
6 Select chart location and click Finish.

3.9 Modifying a Chart

Once a chart has been created, it can be edited by clicking the chart or a chart element to select it. When the black handles are displayed, Chart appears on the Menu bar with drop-down options to change the chart type, source data, chart options, and location. The Format menu changes to display options for formatting the chart or selected chart element.

PROJECT: You will modify the charts created for the *Operating Expenses* worksheet by formatting the legend, changing the font in the chart title, and changing the chart type.

STEPS

1 With Excel S3-04 open, click the mouse pointer inside the legend in the pie chart.

> Black handles display around the legend indicating the legend element is selected. Figure E3.4 shows some of the elements that can be formatted in a chart.

2 Click Format and then Selected Legend.

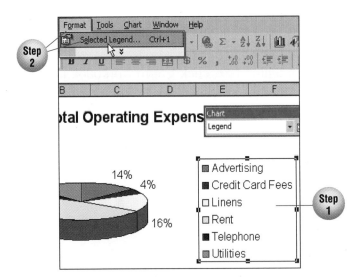

3 With the Patterns tab selected in the Format Legend dialog box, click None in the Border section and then click OK.

> This will remove the border from around the legend.

④ Right-click the chart title and then click F<u>o</u>rmat Chart Title at the shortcut menu.

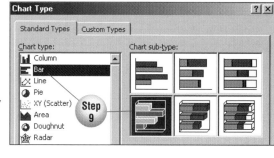
Step 4

⑤ Click the Font tab in the Format Chart Title dialog box.

⑥ Change the font to 20-point Garamond Bold and then click OK.

> Choose another font such as Times New Roman if Garamond is not available on your system.

⑦ Click the *Chart1* tab to display the column chart.

⑧ Click <u>C</u>hart and then Chart T<u>y</u>pe.

⑨ Click *Bar* in the <u>C</u>hart type list box, click the first chart in the second row in the Chart sub-<u>t</u>ype section (Clustered bar with a 3-D visual effect), and then click OK.

Chart Type
Standard Types | Custom Types
<u>C</u>hart type: | Chart sub-<u>t</u>ype:
Column
Bar
Line
Pie
XY (Scatter)
Area
Doughnut
Radar
Step 9

⑩ Preview and print the bar chart.

⑪ Save Excel S3-04.

FIGURE E3.4 Chart Element Formatting

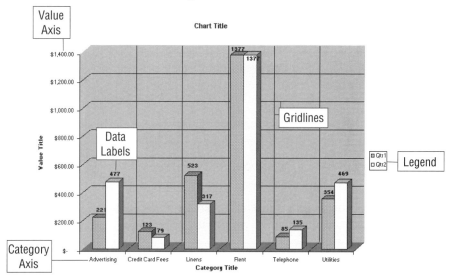

In Addition

Chart Elements

The chart shown in Figure E3.4 illustrates some of the elements that can be added or formatted in a chart. Double-clicking a chart element will open a dialog box with formatting options available for the selected element.

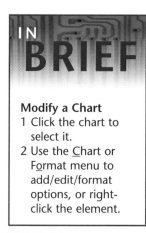
IN BRIEF

Modify a Chart
1 Click the chart to select it.
2 Use the <u>C</u>hart or F<u>o</u>rmat menu to add/edit/format options, or right-click the element.

3.10 Inserting Pictures

Microsoft Office contains a clip art gallery containing pictures that can be inserted into worksheets. Once a picture has been inserted, it can be moved, resized, or deleted. The Clip Art Task Pane allows you to view images in the gallery and insert them into the worksheet with a single click. If you are connected to the Internet you can use the *Clips Online* link in the Insert Clip Art Task Pane to access the Microsoft Office Design Gallery Live. This Web site contains additional images that can be downloaded to your computer.

PROJECT: You will add two clip art images to the top of the worksheet to enhance its appearance. After inserting the images, you will resize and move them.

S T E P S

1. With Excel S3-04 open, click the *Sheet1* tab to display the worksheet and chart.

2. Insert 4 rows above row 1 and then make A1 the active cell.

3. Click Insert, point to Picture, and then click Clip Art.

    The Insert Clip Art Task Pane opens at the right side of the worksheet area.

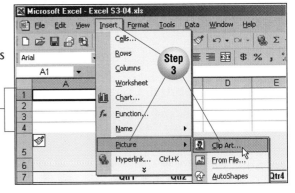

4. Click in the Search text: text box in the Search For section of the Insert Clip Art Task Pane, key **flowers**, and then click Search.

    Available images that have the keyword *flowers* associated with them display in the Results section of the Insert Clip Art Task Pane.

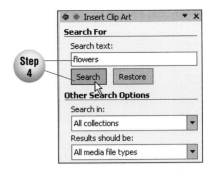

5. Position the mouse pointer over the picture shown below and then click the mouse once.

    The picture is inserted in the worksheet starting at A1 and the Picture toolbar appears.

> **PROBLEM?** Select an alternate picture if the image shown is not available on your system.

6. Click the Close button ☒ in the upper right corner of the Picture toolbar.

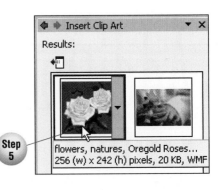

(7) Position the pointer on the white sizing handle at the bottom right corner of the image until the pointer changes to a double-headed diagonal arrow. Hold down the left mouse button and drag the pointer up and to the left until the picture fits within the first four rows above the worksheet title.

(8) Drag the right middle sizing handle until the picture fits the width of column A.

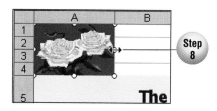

Step 8

(9) Move the pointer inside the image until the four-headed arrow move icon appears attached to the pointer. Hold down the left mouse button, drag the picture until the right edge of the picture is aligned at the right edge of the worksheet, and then release the mouse button.

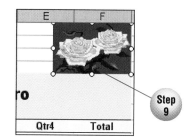

Step 9

(10) Click A1.

(11) Click the Modify button at the bottom of the Results window in the Insert Clip Art Task Pane.

> The Search For and Other Search Options sections of the Insert Clip Art Task Pane are displayed.

(12) Key **business** in the Search text: text box and then click Search.

(13) Insert and resize the image shown at the top left edge of the worksheet. Choose an alternate picture if the image shown is not available.

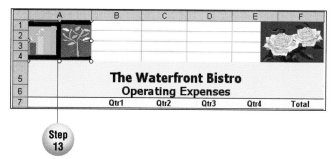

Step 13

(14) Click in any cell to deselect the clip art image.

(15) Click the Close button in the upper right corner of the Insert Clip Art Task Pane.

(16) Print the worksheet.

(17) Save Excel S3-04.

In Addition

Inserting Pictures from a File

Click Insert, point to Picture, and then click From File to insert a picture such as a company logo or other scanned image into a worksheet. Navigate to the location of the file in the Insert Picture dialog box and then double-click the picture file name.

IN BRIEF

Insert a Picture
1 Make the desired cell active.
2 Click Insert, Picture, Clip Art.
3 Key a word that describes the type of picture you want.
4 Scroll the images found in the Results window.
5 Click the picture you want to insert.
6 Close the Insert Clip Art Task Pane.
7 Move and/or resize the picture as required.

3.11 Drawing Arrows and Text Boxes

The Drawing toolbar contains buttons that can be used to draw a variety of shapes such as circles, squares, rectangles, lines, arrows, and text boxes. Draw arrows or text boxes to add emphasis or insert explanatory notes in a worksheet. The AutoShapes button displays a pop-up menu in which palettes of shapes are grouped into categories such as Lines, Basic Shapes, and Block Arrows.

PROJECT: You will draw an arrow and text box to insert an explanatory note regarding the rent increase in the *Operating Expenses* worksheet.

STEPS

① With Excel S3-04 open, click View, point to Toolbars, and then click Drawing to display the Drawing toolbar shown in Figure E3.5.

> Skip step 1 if the Drawing toolbar is already visible.

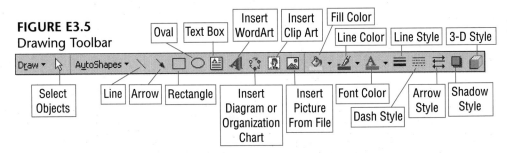

FIGURE E3.5
Drawing Toolbar

Oval | Text Box | Insert WordArt | Insert Clip Art | Fill Color | Line Color | Line Style | 3-D Style

Select Objects | Line | Arrow | Rectangle | Insert Diagram or Organization Chart | Insert Picture From File | Font Color | Dash Style | Arrow Style | Shadow Style

② Click the Arrow button ⬛ on the Drawing toolbar.

> When an object tool has been selected, the pointer changes to a crosshairs ⊞.
> To draw an objcct, position the crosshairs where you want the object to start, hold down the left mouse button, and then drag the crosshairs to the desired ending point.

③ Position the crosshairs near the bottom boundary of D16. Hold down the left mouse button and drag the crosshairs up toward the value *1,515.00* in E11, and then release the left mouse button.

PROBLEM ❓
If you do not like the way the arrow turns out, press Delete to delete the arrow, then click the Arrow button and try again.

Qtr3	Qtr4
$ 358.00	$ 583.00
117.00	168.00
468.00	611.00
1,377.00	1,515.00
164.00	223.00
322.00	409.00
$ 2,806.00	$ 3,509.00

④ Click the Text Box button ⬛ on the Drawing toolbar.

> When the Text Box tool has been selected, the pointer changes to a downward-pointing arrow ⬇.

Step 3

Position crosshairs here, then drag up toward Ell.

5 Position the pointer at the top left boundary of D17 and then drag the pointer down and to the right to draw the text box as shown in the illustration.

> An insertion point appears inside the box when you release the left mouse button indicating you can begin keying the text.

6 Key **A 10% increase!** inside the text box.

7 Click outside the text box object to deselect it.

8 Position the mouse pointer over the border of the text box until the pointer changes to display the four-headed arrow icon attached to it, and then click the left mouse button.

> This selects the text box object. Eight white sizing handles should display around the text box along with a thick gray border.

9 Click the Font Color button on the Drawing toolbar.

> This changes the color of the text inside the box to Red.

PROBLEM?

> Font Color button does not display Red? Click the down-pointing triangle to the right of the button and select Red from the color palette.

10 Click the Line Color button 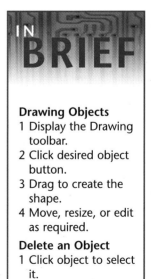 on the Drawing toolbar.

> This changes the line color of the text box border to Blue.

11 Resize the text box by dragging the bottom right corner sizing handle in until the text box border is just right of and below the text, and then click outside the object to deselect the text box.

12 Save Excel S3-04.

13 Print the worksheet and then close Excel S3-04.

In Addition

AutoShapes

The AutoShapes button on the Drawing toolbar contains palettes of shapes grouped into the categories Lines, Connectors, Basic Shapes, Block Arrows, Flowchart, Stars and Banners, and Callouts. Point to a category to view a variety of objects that can be drawn. If space permits, use an AutoShape to add interest to a worksheet. The Block Arrows palette is shown at the right.

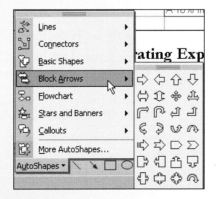

In BRIEF

Drawing Objects
1 Display the Drawing toolbar.
2 Click desired object button.
3 Drag to create the shape.
4 Move, resize, or edit as required.

Delete an Object
1 Click object to select it.
2 Press Delete.

FEATURES SUMMARY

Feature	Button	Menu	Keyboard
Create a chart		Insert, Chart	F11
Draw an arrow			
Draw a text box			
Drawing toolbar		View, Toolbars, Drawing	
Insert a function		Insert, Function	
Insert a picture		Insert, Picture, Clip Art	
Page Setup dialog box		File, Page Setup	
Print dialog box		File, Print	Ctrl + P
Print Preview		File, Print Preview	

PROCEDURES CHECK

Completion: In the space provided at the right, indicate the correct term or command.

1. AVERAGE, MAX, and MIN are some of the functions grouped in this category in the Insert Function dialog box.
2. The date January 1, 1900, is this serial number in Excel.
3. This Date and Time function inserts today's date in the active cell.
4. The financial function PMT returns a monthly payment based on constant payments, a constant interest rate, and this.
5. The IF function returns one of two values in a cell based on the result of this test.
6. Display this window to view how the worksheet will look when printed.
7. To center a worksheet horizontally and vertically, click this tab in the Page Setup dialog box.
8. A header is text that prints here.
9. A worksheet can be scaled to print on a specific number of pages with this option in the Page Setup dialog box.
10. Click Percentage in this tab in the Chart Options dialog box to display the percentage of 100 represented by each slice of a pie chart.
11. Display this dialog box to change the chart title after the chart has been created.

12. Do this action with the mouse over a chart to display the black handles. _____

13. Click this button below the Results window in the Clip Art Task Pane to search for a different picture. _____

14. Display this toolbar to create a text box in the worksheet. _____

15. Write the IF function to calculate a sales bonus given the following criteria:
    • sales bonuses are paid at the rate of 8% for sales over $1 million
    • sales bonuses are paid at the rate of 5% for sales less than or equal to $1 million
    • assume the sales amount is in B3

    _____

16. Write the PMT function to calculate a loan payment given the following criteria:
    • the interest rate per annum is in C5
    • the term of the loan in months is in C6
    • the amount of money borrowed is in C7

    _____

SKILLS REVIEW

Activity 1: INSERTING STATISTICAL FUNCTIONS

1 Open WB Expenses.
2 Save the workbook and name it Excel S3-R1.
3 Make A15 the active cell.
4 Key **Average Expense** and then press Enter.
5 Key **Maximum Expense** and then press Enter.
6 Key **Minimum Expense** and then press Enter.
7 Increase the width of column A to *16.00 (117 pixels)*.
8 Make B15 the active cell and then create the formula *=AVERAGE(B4:B9)*.
9 Make B16 the active cell and then create the formula *=MAX(B4:B9)*.
10 Make B17 the active cell and then create the formula *=MIN(B4:B9)*.
11 Copy the formulas in B15:B17 to C15:F17.
12 Save Excel S3-R1.

Activity 2: CHANGING PRINT OPTIONS

1 With Excel S3-R1 open, display the Page Setup dialog box.
2 Change the top margin to 2 inches and the left margin to 1.5 inches.
3 Create a custom header that will print your first and last names at the left margin, and the current date and time at the right margin.
4 Create a custom footer that will print the word *Page* followed by the page number at the left margin and the file name at the right margin.
5 Turn on the gridlines.
6 Display the worksheet in Print Preview.
7 Close the Print Preview window.
8 Save and then print Excel S3-R1.

Activity 3: USING DATE FUNCTIONS

1 With Excel S3-R1 open, make A19 the active cell.
2 Key **Creation Date** and then press the right arrow key.
3 With B19 the active cell, use the NOW function to insert the current date.
4 Format B19 to display the date in the format *3/14/2001*.
5 Change the width of column B to *10.57 (79 pixels)*.
6 Make A20 the active cell.
7 Key **Next Revision Date** and then press the right arrow key.
8 With B20 the active cell, key the formula **=B19+360** and then press Enter.
9 Save Excel S3-R1.

Activity 4: USING THE IF FUNCTION

1 With Excel S3-R1 open, insert two rows above row 19.
2 Make A19 the active cell.
3 Key **Expense Target**, press Alt + Enter, key **Variance**, and then press Enter.
4 Dana Hirsch, manager of The Waterfront Bistro, has set a quarterly target of $2,850.00 for the total expenses. Dana wants you to create a formula to show the amount over target a quarter's total expenses are, if they have exceeded this target amount. Make B19 the active cell and then key the following IF function:
   =IF(B11>2850,B11-2850,0)
5 Drag the fill handle from B19 to C19:E19.
6 In the space provided, write the values displayed as the results in the cells indicated.
   B19 _____
   C19 _____
   D19 _____
   E19 _____
7 In the space provided, write in your own words a brief explanation of the IF function entered in B19.

_____

_____

_____

8 Assume that Dana Hirsch has changed the expense target to a different amount for each quarter. The revised targets are: *Qtr1–2700; Qtr2–2800; Qtr3–2900; Qtr 4–3100*. Revise the IF functions in B19:E19 to reflect these new targets.
9 Save, print, and then close Excel S3-R1.

Activity 5: CREATING A CHART; INSERTING A PICTURE; DRAWING AN ARROW AND TEXT BOX

1 Open WB Cost of Sales.
2 Save the workbook with Save As and name it Excel S3-R2.
3 Create a 3-D column chart in its own sheet that will present each cost of sales item for the four quarters. Include an appropriate chart title. You determine what other chart elements to include that will make the chart easy to interpret.
4 Draw an arrow pointing to the column in the chart representing Wages & Benefits for the fourth quarter. Create a text box anchored to the end of the arrow and then key the following text inside the box:

   Includes 5% increase in benefit plan from National Life Insurance

5 Insert a clip art image in the worksheet starting in A12 and size it accordingly. You determine an appropriate image to insert.
6 Save Excel S3-R2.
7 Print the entire workbook and then close Excel S3-R2.

PERFORMANCE PLUS

Activity 1: USING STATISTICAL AND IF FUNCTIONS

1 Alex Torres, manager of the Toronto office for First Choice Travel, has started a worksheet to calculate sales commission for the Toronto sales agents. First Choice Travel has implemented a new bonus commission based upon the number of cruises booked. Alex has asked for your help in writing the correct formulas to calculate the commission and analyze the results.
2 Open FCT Commission.
3 Save the workbook and name it Excel S3-P1.
4 Create a formula to calculate the commission for T. Sanderson in D5 using the following criteria:
   • sales agents are paid 1.5% of the total value of their travel bookings for zero to four cruise bookings.
   • a sales agent who has sold five or more cruises will receive 1.75%.
5 Copy the formula to the remaining rows in column D.
6 Calculate the total commissions.
7 Format the values as necessary.
8 Enter appropriate labels and create formulas to calculate the average, maximum, and minimum commissions below the total row.
9 Save, print, and then close Excel S3-P1.

Activity 2: CHANGING PRINT OPTIONS; USING DATE FORMULAS

1 You are the assistant to Cal Rubine, chair of the Theatre Arts Division at Niagara Peninsula College. The two co-op consultants have entered their grades for the work term placements into separate worksheets in the same workbook.
2 Open NPC Co-op.
3 Save the workbook and name it Excel S3-P2.
4 Click the Performance Threads worksheet tab to display the work term placement information for the students who were placed there during the winter semester of 2003.
5 Key a formula in H4 that will add 12 days to the entry in the *Date Co-op Report Received* column.
6 Copy the formula to the remaining rows in column H.
7 Set the following print options:
   a Create a header that will print your name at the left margin and the current date at the right margin.
   b Change the top margin to 2.5 and center the worksheet horizontally.
   c Change the orientation to landscape.
8 Save Excel S3-P2.
9 Print the *Performance Threads* worksheet.
10 Close Excel S3-P2.

Activity 3: APPLYING THE PMT FUNCTION

1 You are the assistant to Sam Vestering, manager of North American Distribution for Worldwide Enterprises. Sam has entered in a workbook details for a proposed building loan and has asked you to enter the formula to calculate the monthly loan payments.
2 Open WE Loan.
3 Save the workbook and name it Excel S3-P3.
4 Enter the formula to calculate the monthly payment in the *New Building Loan* worksheet.
5 Save Excel S3-P3.
6 Print and then close Excel S3-P3.

Activity 4: CREATING AND FORMATTING CHARTS; DRAWING AN ARROW AND TEXT BOX

1 Cal Rubine, chair of the Theatre Arts Division at Niagara Peninsula College, has asked you to create charts from the grades analysis report to present at a divisional meeting. After reviewing the grades, you decide to create a line chart depicting the grades for all of the courses and a pie chart summarizing the total grades.
2 Open NPC Grades.
3 Save the workbook and name it Excel S3-P4.
4 Create a line chart in its own sheet that will display the A+ through F grades for each course. Include an appropriate chart title. You determine what other chart elements to include that will make the chart easy to interpret.
5 Create a 3-D pie chart that will display the total of each grade as a percentage of 100. *(Hint: Select the ranges B4:G4 and B12:G12 before starting the Chart Wizard.)* Include an appropriate chart title. Place the pie chart at the bottom of the *Grades* worksheet starting in row 14.

6 Resize the chart to extend its width to the right edge of column H and the height to the bottom boundary of row 30.

7 Draw an arrow pointing to the F slice in the pie chart. Create a text box at the end of the arrow containing the text *Lowest attrition since 1997!*

8 If necessary, resize the arrow and text box.

9 Change the font color of the text inside the text box to Red.

10 Change the line color of the border of the text box to Blue.

11 Save Excel S3-P4.

12 Print the entire workbook.

13 Close Excel S3-P4.

Activity 5: INSERTING A PICTURE

1 Melissa Gehring, manager of the Los Angeles office for First Choice Travel, has prepared a worksheet listing European destinations and the current package pricing options. Melissa has requested that you enhance the worksheet with clip art and formatting before she presents it at the next staff meeting.

2 Open FCT Europe.

3 Save the workbook and name it Excel S3-P5.

4 Insert an appropriate clip art image at the top right of the worksheet.

5 Increase the height of row 8 to *27.00 (36 pixels)*.

6 Apply the following formatting attributes to the range A7:G8.
   • 11-point Times New Roman Bold
   • Pale blue fill color
   • Center align

7 Format the values in B9:G17 to Currency Style.

8 If necessary, adjust column widths.

9 Apply other formatting attributes that would enhance the appearance of the remainder of the worksheet.

10 Save Excel S3-P5.

11 Print and then close Excel S3-P5.

Activity 6: FINDING INFORMATION ON CREATING WORDART

1 Use Excel's Help feature to find information on how to create a WordArt object in a worksheet.

2 Open FCT Europe.

3 Save the workbook and name it Excel S3-P6.

4 Create a WordArt object at the top right of the worksheet that will display the text *"Europe this summer!"*

5 Resize, move, and format the WordArt object as desired.

6 Save Excel S3-P6.

7 Print and then close Excel S3-P6.

Activity 7: SEARCHING FOR VACATION DESTINATIONS

1   You are trying to choose among vacation alternatives. You decide to use the Internet to locate information on three cities that you would like to visit. Look for detailed travel information such as round-trip airfare, hotel, car rental, and currency exchange.

2   Create an Excel workbook that compares the travel costs for the three cities you researched.

3   Apply formatting enhancements to the worksheet.

4   Create a chart that graphs the total cost of each vacation destination as an object below the worksheet.

5   Add and format chart elements to make the chart easy to interpret.

6   Draw an arrow and text box to the total cost for the vacation destination that you have chosen. Key the text **My Choice!** in the text box.

7   Save the workbook and name it Excel S3-P7.

8   Print and then close Excel S3-P7.

EXCEL

Working with Multiple Worksheets and Managing Files

Using multiple worksheets in a workbook is often a logical way to organize large amounts of data. Formulas can be created that reference cells in other worksheets within the same workbook or within another workbook. One or more ranges can be defined as the print area when you do not require the entire worksheet printed. Styles, creating a workbook from a template, creating and previewing Web pages, filtering lists, locating an existing workbook, creating a new folder, inserting and editing comments, and participating in a Web discussion are some of the other features you will explore. In this section you will learn the skills and complete the projects described here.

 Note: Before beginning this section, delete the Excel S3 *folder on your disk. Next, copy to your disk the* Excel S4 *subfolder from the* Excel *folder on the CD that accompanies this textbook, and then make* Excel S4 *the active folder.*

Skills

- Insert, delete, rename, move, and copy a worksheet
- Link worksheets
- Create 3-D references in formulas
- Print multiple worksheets
- Set and clear a print area
- Create a new workbook using a template
- Define a style
- Apply and remove a style
- Save a worksheet as a Web page
- View a worksheet in Web Page Preview
- Insert and edit a hyperlink
- Filter a list using AutoFilter
- Locate and open an existing workbook
- Create a folder
- Move a file to a folder
- Insert and edit comments
- Create and respond to discussion comments

Projects

 Complete the quarterly sales report and the payroll report; create an invoice to Performance Threads and First Choice Travel using a template; format using styles; save an employee schedule and a sales worksheet as a Web page and insert hyperlinks; print a list of inventory items that had no purchases in the month of April; insert comments to the quarterly sales report and create discussion comments for the operating expenses workbook.

 Create a summary worksheet for the *Theatre Arts Co-op Work Term Placements* report.

Performance Threads — Theatrical Fabrics, Costumes and Supplies — Format a costume production schedule using styles and then save the schedule as a Web page; produce a list of costumes with a final delivery date of July 5; insert comments in the production schedule in preparation for the design team meeting.

4.1 Inserting, Deleting, and Renaming a Worksheet

A new workbook initially contains three sheets named *Sheet1, Sheet2,* and *Sheet3*. Additional sheets can be added or deleted as needed. Organizing large amounts of data by grouping related topics in individual worksheets makes the task of creating, editing, and analyzing data more manageable. For example, a teacher could record test grades in one worksheet and assignment grades in another. A summary sheet at the beginning or end of the workbook would be used to consolidate the test and assignment grades and calculate a final mark. By breaking down the data into smaller units, the teacher is able to view, enter, and edit cells quickly.

PROJECT: Dana Hirsch, manager of The Waterfront Bistro, has asked you to complete the *Quarterly Sales* report. To begin this project, a fourth quarter and a summary sheet need to be inserted and the sheet tabs renamed.

STEPS

1 Open WB Quarterly Sales.

2 Save the workbook and name it Excel S4-01.

3 Click the *Qtr2* tab and then view the worksheet.

Step 3

4 Click the *Sheet3* tab and then view the worksheet.

The quarterly sales report has been organized with each quarter's sales in a separate worksheet. In the next step you will insert a worksheet for the fourth quarter.

Step 4

5 Click Insert and then Worksheet.

New worksheets are inserted to the left of the active worksheet. In the next step you will insert at the beginning of the workbook a new worksheet that will be used to summarize the sales data from the four quarters.

New Worksheet Created in Step 5

6 Right-click the *Qtr1* tab.

Right-clicking a worksheet tab activates the worksheet and displays the worksheet shortcut menu.

Step 7

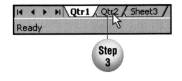

Step 6

7 Click Insert at the shortcut menu.

8 With *Worksheet* already selected in the General tab in the Insert dialog box, click OK.

The Insert dialog box also contains icons to insert a chart, a macro, an international macro sheet, and a dialog box.

9 Insert another worksheet in front of *Sheet2*.

Six worksheets now exist in Excel S4-01: *Sheet4, Sheet2, Qtr1, Qtr2, Sheet1,* and *Sheet3*.

10 Right-click the *Sheet1* tab and then click <u>D</u>elete at the shortcut menu.

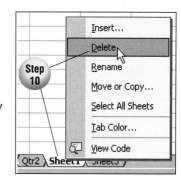

> You can also click <u>E</u>dit and then Delete Sheet to delete the active worksheet from the workbook. If the worksheet selected for deletion contains data, a message box will appear warning you that data may exist in the sheet. Click the Delete button in the Microsoft Excel message box to confirm the deletion. Undo does not restore a deleted sheet.

11 Right-click the *Sheet4* tab and then click <u>R</u>ename at the shortcut menu.

> This selects the current worksheet name in the sheet tab.

12 Key **Summary** and then press Enter.

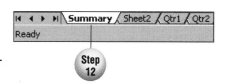

13 Double-click the *Sheet3* tab.

> You can also rename a worksheet by double-clicking the sheet tab.

14 Key **Qtr3** and then press Enter.

15 Save Excel S4-01.

In Addition

Tab Scrolling Buttons

The tab scrolling buttons are located at the left edge of the horizontal scroll bar as shown below. Use these buttons to scroll the worksheet tabs if there are more tabs than currently displayed. Drag the tab split box to the right or left to increase or decrease the number of worksheet tabs displayed or to change the size of the horizontal scroll bar.

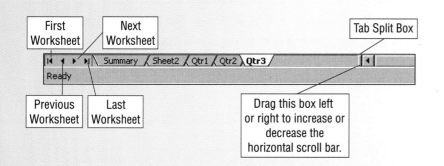

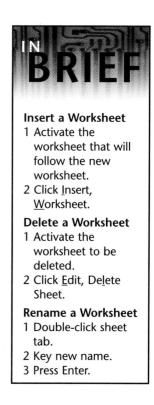

Insert a Worksheet
1 Activate the worksheet that will follow the new worksheet.
2 Click <u>I</u>nsert, <u>W</u>orksheet.

Delete a Worksheet
1 Activate the worksheet to be deleted.
2 Click <u>E</u>dit, De<u>l</u>ete Sheet.

Rename a Worksheet
1 Double-click sheet tab.
2 Key new name.
3 Press Enter.

4.2 Moving and Copying a Worksheet

Drag a sheet tab to move a worksheet to a different position within the open workbook. Hold down Ctrl while dragging a worksheet tab to copy it. Worksheets can also be copied or moved from one workbook to another by opening the Move or Copy dialog box. Exercise caution when moving or copying a worksheet, since calculations may become inaccurate after the worksheet has been repositioned or copied.

PROJECT: Continue your work on the *Quarterly Sales* report. You will copy the *Qtr3* worksheet to create a worksheet for the fourth quarter, since copying will duplicate the labels and formatting. After copying *Qtr3*, you will rename the worksheet, delete the *Qtr3* data, and then enter the *Qtr4* sales. You will move the *Summary* worksheet to the end of the workbook after the four quarters.

STEPS

1. With Excel S4-01 open, delete *Sheet2* from the workbook.

2. Click *Qtr3* to make it the active worksheet.

3. Position the mouse pointer over the *Qtr3* tab, hold down Ctrl and drag the pointer right to the gray area in the scroll bar, release the mouse button, and then release the Ctrl key.

   A black triangle indicates the position where the worksheet will be placed.

   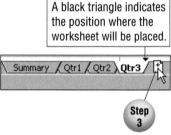

   Step 3

   > As you drag the pointer to the right a black down-pointing triangle and a white page with a plus sign display with the pointer, indicating the position where the copied worksheet will be placed. The copied worksheet is labeled the same as the source worksheet with *(2)* added to the end of the name.

4. Rename *Qtr3 (2)* as *Qtr4*.

5. With *Qtr4* the active worksheet, clear the contents only of the following ranges:

   B4:D6
   B8:D10
   B12:D14

6. Change B3 from *July* to *October;* C3 from *August* to *November;* and D3 from *September* to *December*.

   > The worksheet is now cleared of the third quarter's data. All of the total cells have dashes displayed in them. As new data is keyed, the totals will automatically update.

7. Enter the data for the fourth quarter as shown in Figure E4.1. You do not need to key the dollar symbols, commas, or zeros after decimals since the cells are already formatted. Enter a zero in the cells displayed with a dash.

FIGURE E4.1 Data for Fourth Quarter

	A	B	C	D	E
		The Waterfront Bistro			
		Quarterly Sales Report			
		October	**November**	**December**	**Quarter Total**
4	Food - Dining Room	$ 33,124.00	$ 34,168.00	$ 38,981.00	$ 106,273.00
5	Food - Patio	-	-	-	-
6	Food - Catering	17,623.00	18,234.00	26,691.00	62,548.00
7	**Total Food**	**50,747.00**	**52,402.00**	**65,672.00**	**168,821.00**
8	Beverage - Dining Room	3,147.00	3,217.00	3,342.00	9,706.00
9	Beverage - Patio	-	-	-	-
10	Beverage - Catering	1,672.00	1,734.00	2,716.00	6,122.00
11	**Total Beverage**	**4,819.00**	**4,951.00**	**6,058.00**	**15,828.00**
12	Beer & Liquor - Dining Room	3,416.00	3,571.00	4,085.00	11,072.00
13	Beer & Liquor - Patio	-	-	-	-
14	Beer & Liquor - Catering	1,942.00	1,938.00	3,096.00	6,976.00
15	**Total Beer & Liquor**	**5,358.00**	**5,509.00**	**7,181.00**	**18,048.00**

8 Click *Summary* to make it the active worksheet.

9 Position the pointer over the *Summary* tab, hold down the left mouse button and drag the pointer right to the gray area in the scroll bar after *Qtr4*, and then release the mouse button.

> As you drag the pointer to the right a black down-pointing triangle and a white page display with the pointer, indicating the position where the worksheet will be placed.

10 Save Excel S4-01.

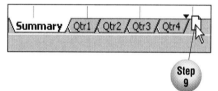

Step 9

In Addition

Move or Copy Dialog Box

In steps 2–3 and 8–9 you copied and moved a worksheet by dragging the sheet tab with the pointer. You can also use the Move or Copy dialog box (shown at the right) to move or copy worksheets within the active workbook or to another open workbook. Select the worksheet to be moved or copied, and then click Edit and Move or Copy Sheet. To move or copy to another open workbook, select the destination file name in the To book drop-down list. Click the worksheet in front of which you want to place the moved or copied worksheet in the Before sheet list box, and click OK to move, or click Create a copy and then click OK to copy.

IN BRIEF

Copy a Worksheet
1 Activate the source worksheet.
2 Hold down Ctrl key.
3 Drag sheet tab to position for copied sheet.

Move a Worksheet
1 Activate the worksheet to be moved.
2 Drag sheet tab to new position.

4.3 Linking Worksheets; Using 3-D References; Formatting Sheet Tabs

Linking worksheets within the same workbook or between different workbooks involves entering a formula that references a cell containing the source data. If the source data changes, the cell that is linked to the source will automatically update to reflect the change. A formula with 3-D references is used to consolidate data from several worksheets into one worksheet. Sheet tabs can have color applied to them which can help you to visually organize worksheets.

PROJECT: The *Summary* worksheet is the last worksheet to be completed in the *Quarterly Sales* report. You will copy labels from the *Qtr4* worksheet to the *Summary* sheet, add labels, enter 3-D formulas that reference the total sales cells in the other worksheets, and link the Gross Profit cell to the *Qtr1* worksheet. Finally, you will add color to the sheet tabs.

STEPS

1. With Excel S4-01 open, make *Qtr1* the active worksheet.

2. Select A4:A22 and then click the Copy button on the Standard toolbar.

3. Make *Summary* the active worksheet, click A4, and then click the Paste button on the Standard toolbar.

4. Increase the width of column A to 25.00 (180 pixels).

5. Make B3 the active cell, key **Total**, press Alt + Enter, key **Sales**, and then press Enter.

6. Bold and center B3.

7. Make *Qtr1* the active worksheet, copy A1, and then paste it to A1 in the *Summary* worksheet.

8. Create the subtitle **Summary Sales Report** in bold, merged and centered in A2:E2.

9. Change the width of column B to 12.00 (89 pixels).

10. Save Excel S4-01.

    Saving the workbook before consolidating data using 3-D references is a good idea in case you encounter difficulties when performing the consolidation.

11. With *Summary* still the active worksheet, make B4 the active cell.

(12) Key **=SUM(Qtr1:Qtr4!E4)** and then click the Enter button on the Formula bar.

The result, *338920*, appears in B4. This is the total of the values in E4 in all of the quarterly sales worksheets. The formula entered in B4 is called a *3-D Reference* since it is referencing a cell spanning two or more worksheets. The argument in the SUM function begins with the range of worksheets *Qtr1:Qtr4* keyed just as you would key a range of cells. The exclamation point is the symbol separating the worksheet range from the cell reference. The argument ends with the cell to be added in the worksheet range.

PROBLEM ?

Cell displays *#NAME?* instead of *338920*? Be sure the formula does not include any spaces. Also confirm that you entered the correct symbols within the formula.

	A	B	C
1		**The Waterfront Bistro**	
2		**Summary Sales Report**	
3		**Total Sales**	
4	Food - Dining Room	338920	
5	Food - Patio		

B4 ▾ *fx* =SUM(Qtr1:Qtr4!E4)

Step 12

(13) Make B5 the active cell.

In steps 14–16 you will enter a 3-D formula using the point-and-click method.

(14) Key **=SUM(**.

(15) Click the *Qtr1* tab, hold down the Shift key, and then click the *Qtr4* tab.

This selects the four quarterly sales worksheets and *Qtr1* is the worksheet now displayed. Notice the formula as it is being added to the Formula bar each time you click the mouse.

(16) Click E5 and then press Enter.

(17) Press the up arrow key to return the active cell back to B5 and then read the formula in the Formula bar, *=SUM(Qtr1:Qtr4!E5)*.

Notice Excel automatically included the closing bracket in the formula when you pressed Enter.

(18) Drag the fill handle from B5 down through B15.

This copies the 3-D formula to the remaining rows.

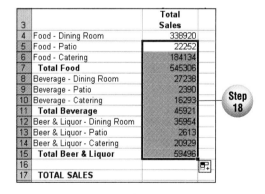

		Total Sales
3		
4	Food - Dining Room	338920
5	Food - Patio	22252
6	Food - Catering	184134
7	**Total Food**	545306
8	Beverage - Dining Room	27238
9	Beverage - Patio	2390
10	Beverage - Catering	16293
11	**Total Beverage**	45921
12	Beer & Liquor - Dining Room	35954
13	Beer & Liquor - Patio	2613
14	Beer & Liquor - Catering	20929
15	**Total Beer & Liquor**	59496
16		
17	**TOTAL SALES**	

Step 18

(19) Make B17 the active cell and then key the formula **=B7+B11+B15**.

(20) Apply the Comma Style format to B4:B15 and then deselect the range.

In the next steps you will use the Format Painter to format the subtotals in the *Summary* sheet.

(21) Make E7 in the *Qtr4* worksheet the active cell.

(22) Double-click the Format Painter button [icon] on the Standard toolbar.

Format Painter copies the formats in the active cell. These formats can then be pasted to other cells in the workbook. Single-click Format Painter to copy formats to a single cell, or double-click Format Painter to copy formats to multiple cells. When Format Painter has been activated, a paintbrush appears with the cell pointer.

(continued)

23 Click the *Summary* tab, click B7, click B11, and then click B15.

24 Click the Format Painter button to turn it off.

25 Use the Format Painter to copy the formats from B4 and B17 in the *Qtr4* worksheet to B4 and B17 in the *Summary* worksheet.

26 Make B21 in the *Summary* sheet the active cell.

> In the next steps you will link the Gross Profit Factor from the *Qtr1* worksheet to the *Summary* sheet.

27 Key the equals sign (=).

28 Click the *Qtr1* tab, click B21, and then press Enter.

> The value *22%* displays in B21 and the formula *=Qtr1!B21* is stored in the active cell. The contents of B21 in the *Summary* sheet are now linked to the contents of B21 in the *Qtr1* worksheet. Any change made to the Gross Profit Factor in the *Qtr1* worksheet will automatically be reflected in the *Summary* worksheet.

	Total Sales
	$ 338,920.00
	22,252.00
	184,134.00
	545,306.00
	27,238.00
	2,390.00
	16,293.00
Step 25 / Step 23	45,921.00
	35,954.00
	2,613.00
	20,929.00
	59,496.00
	$650,723.00

29 With B22 the active cell, key **=B17*B21** and then press Enter.

> Estimated Gross Profit is calculated by multiplying Total Sales (B17) times the Gross Profit Factor (B21).

17	TOTAL SALES		$ 650,723.00
18			
19	Proof Total	Step 28	650,723.00
20			
21	Gross Profit Factor		22%
22	Estimated Gross Profit		143,159.06

Step 30

Step 29

30 Make B19 the active cell and then key a formula that will check the accuracy of the total sales in cell B17. *(Hint: Look at the proof total formulas in the Qtr1–Qtr4 worksheets as an example.)*

31 Right-click the *Summary* tab and then click <u>T</u>ab Color at the shortcut menu.

> Changing the background color of the sheet tabs can help to identify related worksheets or the organizational structure of the workbook.

32 Click the turquoise color button (fourth from left in bottom row) in the Format Tab Color palette and then click OK.

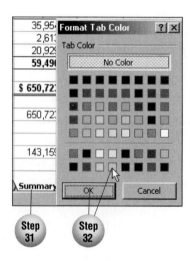

Step 31

Step 32

33 Click the *Qtr1* tab, hold down the Shift key, and then click the *Qtr4* tab.

> Notice the entire background of the *Summary* tab is shaded turquoise when the sheet is not active.

34 Click F<u>o</u>rmat, point to S<u>h</u>eet, and then click <u>T</u>ab Color.

35 Click the yellow color button (third from left in bottom row) and then click OK.

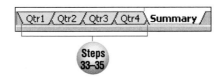

36 Click the *Summary* tab.

37 Save Excel S4-01.

In Addition

3-D References and Moving, Inserting, and Deleting Sheets

Excel performs the following actions to a 3-D formula when worksheets are moved, added, or deleted within the 3-D range in a workbook.

- **Move:** Excel removes the values from the calculation if a worksheet is moved to a location outside the 3-D range.
- **Insert new sheet:** Excel adjusts the 3-D formula to include all values in the same range of cells in the new worksheet(s).
- **Delete:** Excel removes the values from the calculation in the 3-D formula. If the worksheet that is deleted is the beginning or ending sheet in the 3-D range, Excel automatically adjusts the formula to the new range of worksheets.

IN BRIEF

Consolidate Data with 3-D References
1 Activate cell to contain consolidated data.
2 Key the equals sign (=).
3 Click the first worksheet to be included.
4 Hold down Shift and click the last worksheet.
5 Click the cell to be consolidated.
6 Press Enter.

Link Worksheets
1 Activate destination cell.
2 Key the equals sign (=).
3 Click sheet tab for the source data.
4 Click the source cell.
5 Press Enter.

Format Sheet Tabs
1 Right-click sheet tab.
2 Click Tab Color.
3 Click desired color button.
4 Click OK.

EXCEL

4.4 Printing Multiple Worksheets; Setting the Print Area

The Print button on the Standard toolbar will print the active worksheet or multiple worksheets if they have been selected first. If multiple worksheets have not been selected, display the Print dialog box and change the Print what option to Entire workbook. To print a portion of a worksheet, select the cells and then display the Print dialog box. Change the Print what option to Selection. Setting a print area allows you to define one or more ranges of cells to print. Excel saves the print area with the worksheet so that you do not need to define it again the next time you want to print.

PROJECT: Now that the *Quarterly Sales* report is complete, you will experiment with various printing methods.

S T E P S

1 With Excel S4-01 open and the *Summary* sheet active, click the *Qtr1* tab, hold down the Shift key, and then click the *Qtr4* tab.

> This selects all of the worksheets from the first tab through the last tab (*Qtr1–Qtr4*). To select multiple worksheets that are nonadjacent, hold down the Ctrl key while clicking each tab. In topic 3.8, *Creating a Chart,* you printed the chart that was in its own sheet and the worksheet that was used to generate the chart by selecting Entire workbook in the Print what section of the Print dialog box. Entire workbook would have printed all five worksheets in Excel S4-01.

2 Click the Print button.

> The four worksheets print and remain selected.

3 Click the *Summary* tab and then select the cells A3:B17.

> The Print what section of the Print dialog box also contains the option Selection that is used when you want to print only a portion of the active worksheet.

4 Click File and then Print to display the Print dialog box.

5 Click Selection in the Print what section and then click OK.

> Only the cells within A3:B17 print.

6 Click in any cell to deselect A3:B17.

> In the next steps you will define a print area that will be saved with the workbook.

7 Click the *Qtr1* tab, click View and then Page Break Preview.

> PROBLEM ? Click OK if the Welcome to Page Break Preview message box displays.

8 Change the Zoom setting to 85%.

> In Page Break Preview, page breaks are shown as dashed or solid blue lines. You can adjust a page break by dragging the blue line to the desired position. The worksheet can be edited in Page Break Preview.

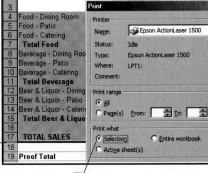

(9) Select A1:E17.

(10) Position the mouse pointer within the selected range, right-click, and then click Set Print Area at the shortcut menu.

Step 9

Step 10

(11) Click in any cell to deselect the range.

> The cells not included in the print area are shown outside the solid blue border in a shaded background.

(12) Click the Print button on the Standard toolbar.

> Only the cells within the print area are printed. In the next steps you will define another print area in a nonadjacent worksheet.

(13) Click the *Summary* tab.

(14) Click View and then Page Break Preview. Change the Zoom setting to 85%.

(15) Select A1:E17. Click File, point to Print Area, and then click Set Print Area.

(16) Click in any cell to deselect the range.

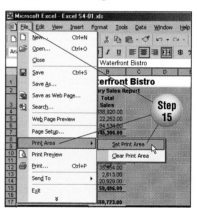

Step 15

(17) Click the *Qtr1* tab, hold down the Ctrl key, and then click the *Summary* tab.

(18) Click the Print Preview button on the Standard toolbar.

> The *Qtr1* worksheet displays in Print Preview and the Status bar at the bottom of the Preview window displays *Page 1 of 2*.

(19) Click Next on the Print Preview toolbar to view the *Summary* worksheet.

(20) Click the Close button on the Print Preview toolbar.

(21) Click the Print button to print the area defined on the *Qtr1* and *Summary* worksheets.

(22) Click the *Qtr3* tab to deselect the two worksheets.

(23) Save and then close Excel S4-01.

In Addition

Clearing the Print Area

The print area is saved with the workbook. Complete the following steps if you decide you want to remove it:

- activate the worksheet with the print area defined.
- click File, point to Print Area, and then click Clear Print Area.

IN BRIEF

Print Multiple Worksheets
1 Select worksheets to be printed.
2 Click Print button.

Print a Selection
1 Select cells to be printed.
2 Click File, Print.
3 Click Selection.
4 Click OK.

Set Print Area
1 Click View, Page Break Preview.
2 Select area to be printed.
3 Click File, Print Area, Set Print Area.

4.5 Creating a Workbook from a Template

Excel includes worksheets that are formatted and have text and formulas created for specific uses such as creating sales invoices, expenses, timecards, and financial statements. These preformatted worksheets are called *templates*. Templates can be customized and saved with a new name to reflect individual company data. Additional templates can be downloaded from the Microsoft Web site.

PROJECT: You will create an invoice to Performance Threads using the Sales Invoice template.

STEPS

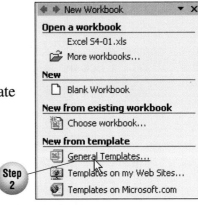

① Click <u>F</u>ile and then <u>N</u>ew.

> The New Workbook Task Pane opens.

② Click *General Templates* in the New from template section in the New Workbook Task Pane.

③ Click the Spreadsheet Solutions tab in the Templates dialog box.

④ Double-click *Sales Invoice*.

PROBLEM? Sales Invoice does not display in the Preview window of the Templates dialog box? Check with your instructor—this feature may not be installed.

⑤ Click the Print Preview button to view the Sales Invoice layout.

⑥ <u>C</u>lose the Print Preview window.

⑦ With the active cell positioned to the right of *Name*, key **Performance Threads** and then press Enter.

> Pressing Enter moves the active cell to the next line (D14) in the template.

⑧ Key **4011 Bridgewater Street** and then click the cell pointer next to *City*.

⑨ Key **Niagara Falls**.

⑩ Click the cell pointer next to *State* and then key **ON**.

⑪ Click the cell pointer next to *ZIP* and then key **L2E 2T6**.

⑫ Click the cell pointer next to *Phone* and then key **(905) 555-2971**.

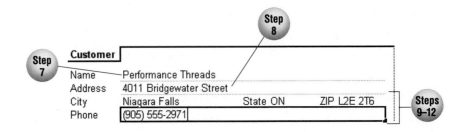

(13) Key the remaining fields in the invoice as shown in Figure E4.2.

> Click the mouse pointer or press Tab or Enter to activate the desired cell before keying text.

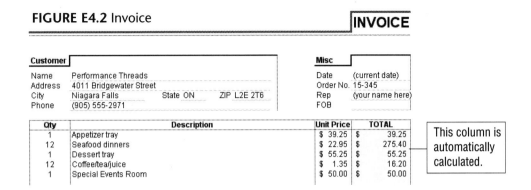

FIGURE E4.2 Invoice

INVOICE

Customer				Misc	
Name	Performance Threads			Date	(current date)
Address	4011 Bridgewater Street			Order No.	15-345
City	Niagara Falls	State ON	ZIP L2E 2T6	Rep	(your name here)
Phone	(905) 555-2971			FOB	

Qty	Description	Unit Price	TOTAL	
1	Appetizer tray	$ 39.25	$	39.25
12	Seafood dinners	$ 22.95	$	275.40
1	Dessert tray	$ 55.25	$	55.25
12	Coffee/tea/juice	$ 1.35	$	16.20
1	Special Events Room	$ 50.00	$	50.00

This column is automatically calculated.

(14) Scroll to the bottom of the invoice to view the remaining entries.

> Notice the cells at the bottom of the invoice labeled *Insert Fine Print Here* and *Insert Farewell Statement Here*. In the next steps you will add information regarding terms of payment and clear the contents of the bottom cell.

(15) Click over the text *Insert Fine Print Here* at the bottom of the invoice.

> The cell C46 is selected and a yellow box appears with instructions on what to do in this cell.

(16) Key **Terms are net 10 days. Interest at the rate of 2% per month will be charged on overdue accounts.**

(17) Click over the text *Insert Farewell Statement Here*.

(18) Click **E**dit, point to Cle**a**r, and then click **C**ontents.

CC #
Expires

Office Use Only

Terms are net 10 days. Interest at the rate of 2% per month will be charged on overdue accounts.

Step 16

Step 18

(19) Scroll to the top of the invoice.

> In the next steps you will enter the name and address for The Waterfront Bistro and the invoice number.

(20) Click over the text *Insert Company Information Here* and then key the following text:

The Waterfront Bistro (press Alt + Enter)
3104 Rivermist Drive (press Alt + Enter)
Buffalo, NY 14280 (press Enter)

(21) Click next to *Invoice No.*, key **2462**, and then press Enter.

(22) Click the Save button on the Standard toolbar.

(23) Key **Excel S4-02** and then press Enter or click **S**ave.

(24) Print the invoice.

(25) Close Excel S4-02.

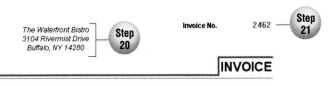

The Waterfront Bistro
3104 Rivermist Drive
Buffalo, NY 14280

Step 20

Invoice No.   2462

Step 21

INVOICE

4.6 Using Styles

A style is a set of predefined formatting attributes that can be applied to a cell. The formatting attributes of a style can include such items as the font, font size, font color, alignment, borders, and numeric format. Using styles to format cells ensures consistent formatting in a workbook. Another advantage to formatting with styles is that all cells will automatically update if the contents of a style have been changed.

PROJECT: You will define, apply, and remove styles in an employee schedule.

STEPS

① Open WB Schedule.

② Save the workbook and name it Excel S4-03.

③ Make A4 the active cell.

> In steps 4–6 you will define a style by applying formats to an existing cell.

④ Apply the following formatting attributes to A4:

Font – Comic Sans MS (choose an alternative font if Comic Sans MS is not available on your system)
Center alignment
Light Turquoise fill color
Dark Blue font color

⑤ With A4 the active cell, click Format and then Style.

⑥ Key **Time-Schedule** in the Style name text box and then click OK.

⑦ Select B4:H4.

> In steps 7–8 you will apply the Time-Schedule style to days of the week.

⑧ Click Format and then Style.

⑨ Click the down-pointing triangle to the right of the Style name text box, click *Time-Schedule* in the drop-down list, and then click OK.

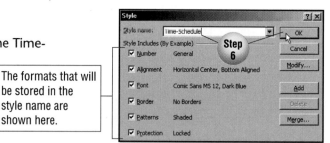

The formats that will be stored in the style name are shown here.

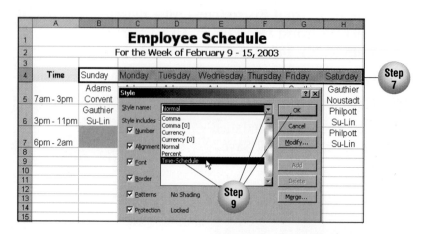

10 Select A5:A7 and then apply the Time-Schedule style.

11 With A5:A7 still selected, click Format and then Style.

12 Click the down-pointing triangle to the right of the Style name text box, click *Normal* in the drop-down list, and then click OK.

> This removes the Time-Schedule style from the selected cells by restoring the default settings.

13 Click the Undo button to reapply the Time-Schedule style back to A5:A7.

14 Click on any cell that has the Time-Schedule style applied.

> In the next steps you will modify the Time-Schedule style and see the immediate effect on the worksheet.

15 Click Format and then Style,

16 Click the down-pointing triangle to the right of the Style name text box and then click *Time-Schedule* in the drop-down list.

17 Click Modify.

18 Click the Patterns tab in the Format Cells dialog box.

19 Click the pale green color button (fourth from left in the fifth row) and then click OK.

20 Click OK to close the Style dialog box.

> The cells with the Time-Schedule style applied to them immediately update to reflect the new color setting.

Steps 14–20
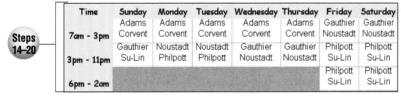

Time	Sunday	Monday	Tuesday	Wednesday	Thursday	Friday	Saturday
7am - 3pm	Adams Corvent	Adams Corvent	Adams Corvent	Adams Corvent	Adams Corvent	Gauthier Noustadt	Gauthier Noustadt
3pm - 11pm	Gauthier Su-Lin	Noustadt Philpott	Noustadt Philpott	Gauthier Noustadt	Gauthier Noustadt	Philpott Su-Lin	Philpott Su-Lin
6pm - 2am						Philpott Su-Lin	Philpott Su-Lin

21 Save Excel S4-03.

In Addition

Copying Styles to Another Workbook

Styles you create are saved in the workbook in which they were created. To copy a style from an existing workbook to another workbook, make sure both workbooks are open and activate the workbook into which you want to copy the styles. Display the Style dialog box and then click Merge. In the Merge Styles dialog box, double-click the name of the workbook that contains the styles you want to copy and then click OK.

IN BRIEF

Define a Style
1 Apply desired formatting to a cell.
2 Activate cell containing formats.
3 Click Format, Style.
4 Key a name for the style.
5 Click OK.

Apply a Style
1 Select cells you want to format.
2 Click Format, Style.
3 Click down-pointing triangle next to Style name text box.
4 Click desired style name.
5 Click OK.

4.7 Creating a Web Page from a Worksheet; Inserting and Editing Hyperlinks

A worksheet can be saved as a Web page that can be published on a Web server. Excel worksheets or entire workbooks may be published on a company intranet as a method of distributing the data to employees. Use hyperlinks in a Web page to jump to another file or location on the Internet when the hyperlinked text is clicked.

PROJECT: You will save the employee schedule as a Web page, insert a hyperlink to another worksheet, edit a URL in an existing hyperlink, and preview the worksheets in the browser window.

S T E P S

1 With Excel S4-03 open, click File and then Save as Web Page.

This displays the Save As dialog box with the Save as type option automatically changed to *Web Page (*.htm; *.html)*. The extension *.htm* will automatically be added to the name keyed in the File name text box.

2 Key **Employee Schedule** in the File name text box and then click the Save button.

The option Entire Workbook is selected by default. In a workbook with multiple worksheets, the Web page will contain sheet tabs in a manner similar to the Excel window. To save an individual worksheet only or a group of worksheets within the workbook, select the worksheets before opening the Save As dialog box and then click Selection: Sheet.

3 Click File and then Web Page Preview.

The worksheet is displayed in the default Web browser window as shown in Figure E4.3.

4 Close the browser window.

5 Make B9 the active cell.

6 Key **Next Week's Schedule** and then click the Enter button in the Formula bar.

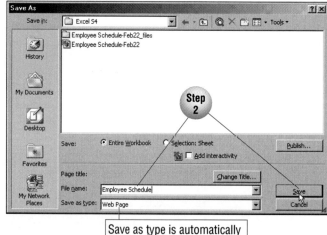

Step 2

Save as type is automatically set to *Web Page*.

FIGURE E4.3 Employee Schedule in Web Browser Window

The Address may vary in your system.

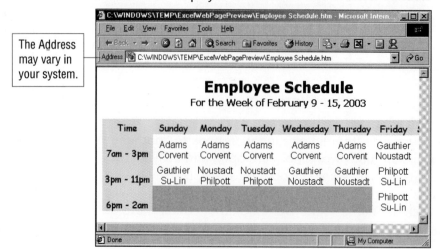

(7) Apply the Normal style to B9. *(The text in B9 is automatically formatted to the Time-Schedule style.)*

> In steps 8–9 you will insert a hyperlink to the employee schedule file for the following week.

(8) With B9 the active cell, click the Insert Hyperlink button 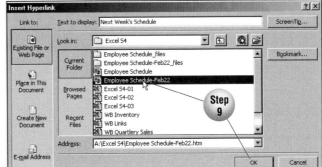 on the Standard toolbar.

(9) Click *Employee Schedule-Feb22* in the file list box and then click OK.

> To hyperlink to a location on the Internet, key the URL for the location in the Address text box.

(10) Display the worksheet in Web Page Preview.

(11) When the worksheet displays in the browser window, scroll to the hyperlinked text *Next Week's Schedule* and then click the text to display the linked file.

(12) After viewing the schedule for the following week, click the Back button in the browser window to return to the previous schedule.

(13) Close the browser window.

(14) Save and then close Employee Schedule-Feb22.htm.

> In the next steps you will open a worksheet that has links already created and edit one of the links that has an error in it.

(15) Open WB Links.

(16) Save the workbook and name it Excel S4-04.

> The Waterfront Bistro created this workbook for their customers to view areas of interest around Buffalo. A customer has reported that the first link to the Web site for the city of Buffalo, New York, does not work.

(17) Position the cell pointer over A9, right-click, and then click Edit Hyperlink at the shortcut menu.

> The Edit Hyperlink dialog box opens with the insertion point positioned in the Address text box. Notice the word *buffalo* is misspelled in the URL.

(18) Click the insertion point within the word *bufaloe*, insert and delete text as required correcting the spelling, and then click OK.

(19) Save Excel S4-04.

(20) Make sure you are connected to the Internet and then click the link in A9 to open the default Web browser and view the Web page.

(21) Click the Back button in the browser window to return to the worksheet.

(22) Close Excel S4-04.

Save as Web Page
1 Click File, Save as Web Page.
2 Key name for Web page.
3 Click Save.

Insert a Hyperlink
1 Select cell.
2 Click Insert, Hyperlink.
3 Key file name or URL.
4 Click OK.

4.8 Filtering Lists Using AutoFilter

In Excel, a list is a worksheet with information set up in rows in which each column represents one unit of similar data called a *field*, and each row is called a *record*. The first row of the list contains labels, which describe the contents in each field (column). The data entered in each cell is called a *field value*. A record (row) contains all of the fields for one unit in the list. For example, a worksheet containing employee names, employee numbers, departments, and salaries would be considered a list. One row, or record, in the list would contain all of the information for one employee. A *filter* is used to display only certain records within the list that meet specified criteria.

PROJECT: Dana Hirsch, manager of The Waterfront Bistro, has asked you to print a list of food inventory items in April that had no purchases and another one that shows those items with only 1 or 2 units purchased.

STEPS

1. Open WB Inventory.

2. Save the workbook and name it Excel S4-05.

3. Make F2 the active cell.

4. Click <u>D</u>ata, point to <u>F</u>ilter, and then click Auto<u>F</u>ilter.

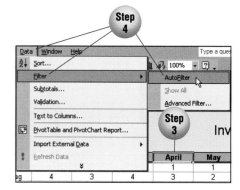

Excel includes the *AutoFilter* feature, which allows you to filter a list by selecting the criteria from a drop-down list. For each column in the list, a button with a down-pointing triangle appears. Click the button in the column that you want to filter by and then click the field value representing the criteria by which Excel should include records. All other records that do not match the selection you click are temporarily removed from the worksheet.

5. Click the down-pointing triangle next to *April* in F2.

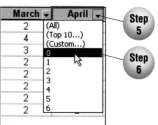

Excel looks in the active column and includes in the drop-down list each unique field value that exists within the column in the worksheet. In addition, the entries *(All)*, *(Top 10)*, and *(Custom)* appear at the top of the list.

6. Click *0* in the drop-down list.

Excel hides any records in the worksheet that have a value other than zero (0) in column F as shown in Figure E4.4. The row numbers of the matching items are displayed in blue and the down-pointing triangle in the column that was used to filter by is also blue. The Status bar shows the message *Filter Mode*. A filtered worksheet can be edited, formatted, charted, or printed.

7. Select A2:F52.

8. Click <u>F</u>ile and then <u>P</u>rint. Click Selectio<u>n</u> in the Print what section of the Print dialog box and then click OK.

9. Click in any cell to deselect A2:F52.

10 Click the down-pointing triangle next to *April* in F2.

11 Click *(All)* in the drop-down list.

> All of the records are redisplayed in the worksheet. In the next steps you will filter the worksheet by more than one criterion.

12 Click the down-pointing triangle next to *April* in column F and then click *(Custom)* in the drop-down list.

> The Custom AutoFilter dialog box appears. This dialog box is used when you want to filter by two criteria.

13 With the insertion point positioned in the white text box next to *equals* in the Show rows where section, key **1**.

14 Click Or.

15 Click the down-pointing triangle next to the white text box below the And and Or option buttons and then click *equals* in the drop-down list.

16 Click in the white text box below *1*, key **2**, and then click OK.

> Only those records with a value of either 1 or 2 in column F are displayed.

17 Select A2:F51 and then print the selected cells.

18 Click in any cell to deselect A2:F51.

19 Click the down-pointing triangle next to *April* in column F and then click *(All)*.

20 Click Data, point to Filter, and then click AutoFilter.

> The buttons with the down-pointing triangles are removed from each column.

21 Save and then close Excel S4-05.

FIGURE E4.4 Filtered Worksheet

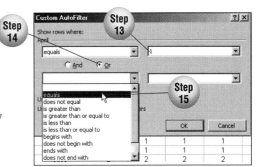

Only records with zero in column F are displayed.

In Addition

Using Wildcards to Filter

A wildcard is a character included in criteria where you do not want to be specific. Excel recognizes two wildcard characters. An asterisk (*) is used to represent any number of unspecified characters and a question mark (?) is used to represent any single character. For example, in the *Inventory Units Purchased* report, suppose you want a list of all of the varieties of peppers. Keying ***peppers** in the Custom AutoFilter dialog box in column A would produce a list of items within column A that had any series of characters before the text *peppers*.

4.9 Locating a Workbook; Creating a New Folder

Once you have been working with Excel for a period of time you will have accumulated several workbook files. On occasion you may not remember the file name of a workbook that you need to open. Excel includes a Search feature in the Open dialog box that can be used to search for files using a variety of criteria. A new folder can be created within Excel using either the Open or Save As dialog box. Organizing your workbooks by creating folders for similar types of files will make the task of finding files faster and easier.

PROJECT: You have forgotten the names of the files that were created for the inventory reports. You will use the Search feature to find all files that contain the text *Inventory*. You will begin organizing your Excel files by creating a new folder and then moving files into the folder.

STEPS

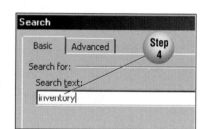

1 Click the New button on the Standard toolbar and then click the Open button to display the Open dialog box.

2 Click the Tools button on the Open dialog box toolbar and then click Search.

3 If necessary, click the Basic tab in the Search dialog box.

4 With the insertion point positioned in the Search text text box, key **inventory**.

> Key text that you know exists in the workbook in the Search text text box. Excel will look in all of the files designated in the Search in locations and list any workbook that contains the specified text in the Results list box.

5 Click the down-pointing triangle in the Search in text box (currently reads *Selected locations*).

> By default, Excel will search *Everywhere*, which includes all disk drives and network locations.

6 Click the check boxes next to *My Network Places* and *Outlook* to deselect those locations.

7 Click the plus symbol next to *My Computer* to expand the folder list. Expand the folder list for the floppy drive. Deselect all locations *except* the location where you store your data files. For example, deselect all locations except *3½ Floppy (A:)* or *My Documents*.

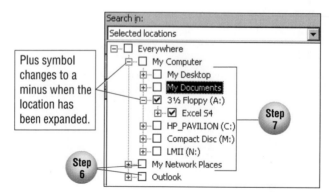

Plus symbol changes to a minus when the location has been expanded.

8 Click in the Search dialog box outside the Search in list to remove the list box.

9 Click the Search button located below the Search in text box.

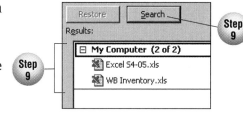
Step 9

> Excel will look for the text *inventory* in each file in the selected locations list. Files that match the criteria display in the Results list box.

Step 9

10 Double-click the file *Excel S4-05*.

> The Search dialog box closes and Excel S4-05 (including the full path) is inserted in the File name text box in the Open dialog box.

11 Click Open.

> In the next steps you will create a new folder and move the files created in section 4 into the newly created folder.

12 Close Excel S4-05. Display the Open dialog box and then click the Create New Folder button [icon] on the Open dialog box toolbar.

Step 12

13 Key **Accounting** and then press Enter or click OK.

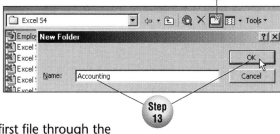

14 Click the Back button [icon] on the Open dialog box toolbar.

Step 13

15 Click *Excel S4-01* in the file list, hold down Shift, and then click *Excel S4-05*.

> This selects all of the files starting with the first file through the last file selected.

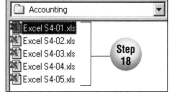

16 Move the arrow pointer inside the selected group of files, right-click, and then click Cut at the shortcut menu.

Step 18

> The icons of the selected files appear dimmed in the file list.

17 Double-click the folder named *Accounting*.

> This changes the active folder in the Open dialog box to *Accounting*.

18 Right-click in the file list area and then click Paste at the shortcut menu.

> The files are pasted in the current folder.

19 Close the Open dialog box.

In Addition

Advanced Search Options

If you know more details about a file, use the Advanced tab in the Search dialog box. You can search for a file based on more than one criterion, based on a file property such as author, creation date, last modified date, size, subject, company, number of pages, template, and so on.

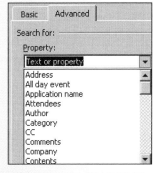

EXCEL

4.10 Inserting and Editing Comments

A comment is additional information that displays in a yellow pop-up box when the cell pointer is positioned over the cell. Comments can be used to provide specific instructions, identify significant information, or add explanatory text to a cell that provides a reader with information that will assist him or her in interpreting or analyzing the data.

PROJECT: Dana Hirsch, manager of The Waterfront Bistro, has asked you to send him the sales summary report. You will insert and edit comments in the *Qtr4* and *Sales Summary* tabs for Dana's review.

STEPS

1. Open Excel S4-01 and then save the workbook as Excel S4-06.

2. Click the *Qtr4* tab.

3. Make D4 the active cell.

4. Click Insert and then Comment.

   A yellow comment box displays anchored to the active cell with the user's name inserted in bold text at the top of the box and a blinking insertion point.

5. Key **This is a 6% increase over last December**.

6. Click in the worksheet outside the comment box.

   The comment box closes and a diagonal red triangle appears in the upper right corner of D4 indicating a comment exists for the cell.

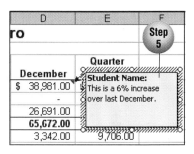

7. Position the cell pointer over B21 and then right-click the mouse.

8. Click Insert Comment at the shortcut menu.

9. Key **Check with accountant to see if this factor should be revised next year**.

10. Click in the worksheet outside the comment box.

11. Hover the cell pointer over D4.

    When you hover the cell pointer over a cell that contains a comment, the comment box appears.

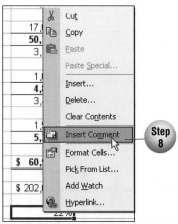

12. Hover the cell pointer over B21.

13. Click the *Summary* tab.

14. Click View and then Normal.

15. Insert a comment in cell B5 that contains the following text:

    Patio sales are down 12% due to inclement weather during the summer months.

    In the next steps you will edit the comment in cell D4 on the Qtr1 tab.

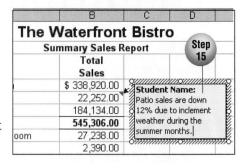

16 Click the *Qtr4* tab.

17 Position the cell pointer over cell D4 and then right-click the mouse.

18 Click <u>E</u>dit Comment at the shortcut menu.

> The yellow comment box appears with the insertion point positioned at the end of the existing text.

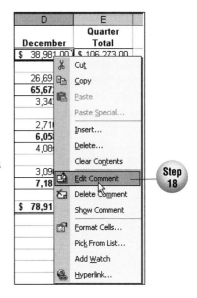

Step 18

19 Use the arrow keys to move the insertion point between *6* and *%*, or click the insertion point, press Backspace to delete the *6*, key **4**, and then click outside the box.

D	E	F
	Quarter	
December	Student Name:	
$ 38,981.00	This is a 4↑% increase over last December.	
-		
26,691.00		
65,672.00		
3,342.00	9,706.00	

Step 19

20 Click <u>V</u>iew and then <u>C</u>omments.

> All of the comments in the worksheet display and the Reviewing toolbar displays.

21 Click the *Summary* tab.

22 Click <u>V</u>iew and then <u>C</u>omments. Click the Close button at the right end of the Reviewing toolbar.

23 Save Excel S4-06.

In Addition

Printing Comments

By default, comments do not print with the worksheet. Comments can be printed as they are displayed in the worksheet or at the end of the worksheet on a separate page. To turn on the printing of comments, click <u>F</u>ile and then Page Set<u>u</u>p. Click the Sheet tab in the Page Setup dialog box. Click the down-pointing triangle to the right of Co<u>m</u>ments in the Print section and then click either *At end of sheet* or *As displayed on sheet*.

4.11 Creating and Responding to Discussion Comments

Microsoft Office XP includes the Web Discussions feature, which provides the ability for multiple users to open a Word document, an Excel workbook, or a PowerPoint presentation and attach comments to the file. The comments appear with the document but are stored on a Web server that has been configured as a *discussion server*. The comments are called *discussions* since each user can attach a response to any comment placed in the file. The comments appear in the file as *a thread,* which is the term used to describe the placement of the

original comment and the attached responses grouped together in hierarchical order.

PROJECT: You will open the *Operating Expenses* workbook, connect to a discussion server, create and then respond to discussion comments.

Note: Check with your instructor before completing this topic. You will need a discussion server address for your school's server, a username, and a password that have been configured for discussion permissions.

STEPS

1 Open WB Operating Expenses.htm. *(You may need to click the Up One Level button ⬆ on the Open dialog box toolbar to return to the file list one level above the* Accounting *folder.)*

2 Save the workbook in the *Accounting* folder and name it Excel S4-07.

> Excel will automatically save the workbook with the file extension .htm.

3 Click Tools, point to Online Collaboration, and then click Web Discussions.

4 Click the Add button in the Discussion Options dialog box.

> **PROBLEM?** Discussion Options dialog box didn't appear? Click the Discussions button on the Web Discussions toolbar and then click Discussion Options.

5 Key **http://servername** (replace *servername* with the address provided by your instructor) in the Type the name of the discussion server your administrator has provided text box in the Add or Edit Discussion Servers dialog box.

6 Click in the You can type any name you want to use as a friendly name for the discussion server text box, key **My Class Discussion Server**, and then click OK.

7 Key your username and password for the discussion server.

> The discussion server name and URL are added to the Select a discussion server text box in the Discussion Options dialog box.

8 Click OK in the Discussion Options dialog box.

> **PROBLEM?** Message box appears with the text *Unable to download data from servername*? Click OK. Click Edit in the Discussion Options dialog box and then check that you keyed the server address correctly. Check with your instructor if the address is keyed correctly.

9 Click the Insert Discussion about the Workbook button 📋 on the Web Discussions toolbar located just above the status bar.

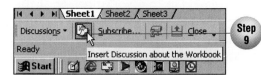

10 With the insertion point positioned in the Discussion subject text box in the Enter Discussion Text dialog box, key **Qtr4 Rent Increase**.

11 Click in the Discussion text text box and then key the following text:

This is a 10% increase. I think we should try to negotiate a new lease with a rent increase that is closer to 4%.

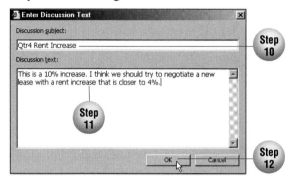

12 Click OK.

The Discussion comment is uploaded to a database file on the server. In a few seconds, the Discussion pane will appear with the Discussion comment inserted as shown in Figure E4.5.

13 Click the Insert Discussion about the Workbook button on the Web Discussions toolbar and then create the following comment:

Discussion subject   **Linen Service Provider**
Discussion text   **Cal is getting quotes from two new suppliers. We should have comparative information within the next two weeks.**

In the next steps you will respond to the comment you created in steps 9–12. Normally, a reply would be posted by another user—you are replying to your own comment for practice to learn the steps.

14 Click the up scroll arrow in the Discussion pane to scroll to the end of the Qtr4 Rent Increase comment.

15 Click the Show a menu of actions button at the end of the comment and then click Reply.

The Enter Discussion Text dialog box appears with the Discussion subject text box already filled in with the subject text *Re: Qtr4 Rent Increase*.

16 With the insertion point already positioned in the Discussion text text box, key the following text and then click OK.

I agree. Let's set up an appointment with the landlord for next week. We should emphasize our 26-year excellent credit history.

The reply text is shown as a *thread* from the original comment in the Discussion pane.

FIGURE E4.5 Worksheet with Web Discussion Pane

17 Click the Discussions button on the Web Discussions toolbar, click Print Discussions, and then click OK in the Print dialog box.

18 Click the Close button on the Web Discussions toolbar.

19 Close Excel S4-07.

FEATURES SUMMARY

Feature	Button	Menu	Keyboard
AutoFilter		Data, Filter, AutoFilter	
Create a folder	🗁		
Delete worksheet		Edit, Delete Sheet	
Discussion comments		Tools, Online Collaboration, Web Discussions	
Format sheet tab		Right-click sheet tab, Tab Color	
Insert a comment		Insert, Comment	
Insert a hyperlink	🔗	Insert, Hyperlink	Ctrl + K
Insert a worksheet		Insert, Worksheet	
Move or copy a worksheet		Edit, Move or Copy Sheet	
Page Break Preview		View, Page Break Preview	
Rename a worksheet		Right-click sheet tab, Rename	
Save as Web Page		File, Save as Web Page	
Search for workbook		Display Open dialog box, Tools, Search	
Style dialog box		Format, Style	
Templates dialog box		File, New	
Web Page Preview		File, Web Page Preview	

PROCEDURES CHECK

Completion: In the space provided at the right, indicate the correct term or command.

1. A new workbook initially contains this many sheets. _____
2. A new worksheet is inserted to this side of the active worksheet. _____
3. Hold down this key while dragging a sheet tab to copy the sheet. _____
4. The formula =*SUM(Expense1:Expense4!G4)* includes this type of reference. _____
5. A worksheet is linked to another worksheet within the same workbook by creating this. _____
6. Change to this view to define a print area that will save one or more ranges to print in a worksheet. _____
7. Worksheets that are preformatted for specific uses, such as creating sales invoices or expenses, are called this. _____

8. Consider storing formatting attributes in this to ensure consistent formatting in a worksheet. _____

9. Worksheets saved as a Web page have this file extension added to the file name. _____

10. Use this preview feature to view a Web page in the default browser window. _____

11. Display this dialog box to enter a file name or URL to jump to when the selected text is clicked in the browser window. _____

12. This mode is active when only certain records that meet a criteria are displayed in the worksheet. _____

13. This feature can be used to assist with locating a workbook. _____

14. Additional information about a cell that appears in a yellow pop-up box when the cell pointer is positioned over the cell is called this. _____

15. This feature allows multiple users to open a workbook and create and respond to comments about the file where the comments are not stored with the original text. _____

16. List the steps you would complete to start a new workbook using the Expense Statement template.

_____

_____

17. List the steps you would complete to locate all of the workbooks stored in the default folder that begin with the text *Finance Department*.

_____

_____

18. List the steps you would complete to create a new folder named *Budgets* within the default folder.

_____

_____

SKILLS REVIEW

Activity 1: INSERTING, DELETING, COPYING, AND RENAMING A WORKSHEET

1 Open WB Payroll.
2 Save the workbook and name it Excel S4-R1 in the *Excel S4* folder.
3 Copy the *Week2* worksheet, positioning the new sheet after *Week3*.
4 Rename the *Week2 (2)* worksheet as *Week4*.
5 Delete the *Week3* worksheet.
6 Copy the *Week2* worksheet, positioning the new sheet between *Week2* and *Week4*.
7 Rename the *Week2 (2)* worksheet as *Week3*.
8 Insert a new worksheet positioned before *Week1* and then rename the worksheet *Summary*.
9 Make *Week3* the active worksheet and then edit the following cells:
      Change E9 from *0* to *5*.
      Change I6 from *6* to *0*.
10 Make *Week4* the active worksheet and then edit the following cells:

Change C11 from *0* to *8*.

Change G11 from *9* to *0*.

11 Save Excel S4-R1.

Activity 2: USING 3-D REFERENCES; LINKING WORKSHEETS; PRINTING MULTIPLE WORKSHEETS

1 With Excel S4-R1 open, copy A1:A2 from any worksheet to A1:A2 in the *Summary* worksheet.

2 Copy A5:A15 from any worksheet to A5:A15 in the *Summary* worksheet.

3 Copy J5:L5 from any worksheet to C5:E5 in the *Summary* worksheet.

4 With *Summary* the active worksheet, create a SUM formula with a 3-D reference in C6 that will total the hours for Adams for all four weeks.

5 Make C6 the active cell and then drag the fill handle down to row 11.

6 Make B15 the active cell and then enter a formula that will link B15 in the *Summary* worksheet to B15 in the *Week1* worksheet.

7 Make cell C3 in *Week1* the active cell and then use the DATE function to enter the date *May 10, 2003*.

8 Key a formula in C4 that will add three days to the date in C3 and then increase the width of column C as needed to display the dates.

9 Complete steps similar to those in 7 and 8 to enter the week ended and payment dates in the remaining worksheets as follows:

C3 in *Week2* **May 17, 2003**

C3 in *Week3* **May 24, 2003**

C3 in *Week4* **May 31, 2003**

10 Make K6 in *Week1* the active cell and then key the formula =**IF(J6>40,J6-40,0)**.

11 Drag the fill handle from K6 down to K11 and then use the AutoSum button to calculate the total overtime hours in D13.

12 Make L6 the active cell and then key the formula =**(J6*$B$15)+(K6*($B$15*.5))**. In your own words, describe what this formula is calculating and why the reference to B15 must be an *absolute reference*.

_____

_____

_____

13 Drag the fill handle from L6 down to L11 and then use the AutoSum button to calculate the total gross pay in L13.

14 Complete the overtime hours and gross pay for *Week2–Week4*. *(Hint: Use the Copy command to copy the IF and Gross Pay formulas from* Week1.*)*

15 Make *Summary* the active worksheet and then enter the 3-D reference formulas in D6 and E6 to consolidate the overtime hours and gross pay for Adams from all four worksheets.

16 Copy the 3-D formulas in D6:E6 to D7:E11.

17 Calculate the totals in C13:E13.

18 Format the *Gross Pay* column to Currency Style.

19 Select A1:A2 and then click the Merge and Center button on the Formatting toolbar. This splits the merged cells.

20 Select A1:E1 and then click the Merge and Center button. Repeat this step for A2:E2.

21 Print all five worksheets.
22 Save and then close Excel S4-R1.

Activity 3: CREATING A WORKBOOK USING A TEMPLATE

1 Start a new workbook using the Sales Invoice template.
2 Complete the customer invoice as follows:
   - First Choice Travel; 4277 Yonge Street; Toronto, ON M4P 2E6; 416-555-9834
   - Order No. – Alex Torres
   - 16 Lunches @13.77
   - 16 Desserts @4.99
   - 16 Beverages @1.68
   - 1 Delivery and Setup @55.00
3 Save the invoice in the *Excel S4* folder and name it Excel S4-R2.
4 Print and then close Excel S4-R2.

Activity 4: CREATING AND APPLYING STYLES

1 Open WB Sales-Feb 15.
2 Save the workbook in the *Excel S4* folder and name it Excel S4-R3.
3 Make B6 the active cell and then apply the following format attributes:
   - Light Yellow fill color
   - Plum font color
   - Italic
4 Create a style named Totals using the formatting in B6.
5 Apply the Totals style to the following ranges:
   - C6:I6
   - B9:I9
   - B12:I12
   - B17:I17
6 Make B14 the active cell and then apply the following format attributes:
   - Light Turquoise fill color
   - Dark Blue font color
   - Italic
7 Create a style named Final_Totals using the formatting in B14.
8 Apply the Final_Totals style to C14:I14.
9 Save Excel S4-R3.

Activity 5: SAVING A WORKSHEET AS A WEB PAGE; VIEWING A WORKSHEET IN WEB PAGE PREVIEW; INSERTING A HYPERLINK; INSERTING COMMENTS

1 With Excel S4-R3 open, save the worksheet as a Web page named Sales-Feb15.
2 Make A19 the active cell and then key **View Quarterly Operating Expenses**.
3 Create a hyperlink in A19 to jump to the file named WB Operating Expenses.htm. *(Hint: You may have to click the Up One Folder button in the Edit Hyperlink dialog box to browse the files in the folder one level up from* Excel Section 4.*)*
4 Save the revised Web page.
5 View the Web page in the default browser window. Click the hyperlinked text to view the WB Operating Expenses Web page.
6 Close the browser window.

7   Insert a comment in B16 that contains the following text:

Check with Dana Hirsch about revising this factor to 19% starting in March due to increased costs.

8   Save, print, and then close Sales-Feb15.

PERFORMANCE PLUS

Activity 1: INSERTING, DELETING, AND RENAMING A WORKSHEET; LINKING WORKSHEETS

1   You are the assistant to Cal Rubine, chair of the Theatre Arts Division at Niagara Peninsula College. The two co-op consultants have entered their grades for the work term placements into separate worksheets in the same workbook. You need to create a worksheet to summarize the data.

2   Open NPC Co-op.

3   Save the workbook in the *Excel Section 4* folder and name it Excel S4-P1.

4   Insert a new worksheet and position it before the *Marquee Productions* worksheet.

5   Rename *Sheet1* as *Grade Summary*.

6   Complete the *Grade summary* worksheet by completing the following tasks:

   a   Copy A3:B7 in the *Marquee Productions* worksheet to A3:B7 in the *Grade Summary* worksheet and then adjust the column widths of columns A and B.

   b   Copy A4:B8 in the *Performance Threads* worksheet to A8:B12 in the *Grade Summary* worksheet.

   c   Copy G3:H3 in the *Marquee Productions* worksheet to C3:D3 in the *Grade Summary* worksheet.

   d   Adjust the column widths of columns C and D and the row height, if necessary.

   e   Link the data in columns C and D of the *Grade Summary* worksheet to the corresponding grades and dates in the *Marquee Productions* and *Performance Threads* worksheets. *(Note: The last five entries in the* Date Co-op Grade Entered *column will display as zero after linking since there is no data in the source cells.)*

   f   Copy the title and subtitle in rows 1 and 2 from the *Marquee Productions* worksheet to the *Grade Summary* worksheet and adjust the format as necessary.

   g   Make any other formatting changes you see fit to the *Grade Summary* worksheet.

7   Save Excel S4-P1.

8   Select all three worksheets and then change the page orientation to landscape.

9   Print all three worksheets and then close Excel S4-P1.

Activity 2: CREATING AND APPLYING STYLES; SAVING A WORKSHEET AS A WEB PAGE; VIEWING A WORKSHEET IN WEB PAGE PREVIEW

1   Bobbie Sinclair, business manager at Performance Threads, needs a costume production schedule posted on the company intranet. You have reviewed the production schedule and have decided that using styles to format the schedule will ensure that consistent formatting attributes are applied to the worksheet before saving it as a Web page.

2   Open PT Costume Schedule.

3   Save the workbook in the *Excel Section 4* folder and name it Excel S4-P2.

4 Make A11 the active cell and then create a style named Headings that will apply the following formatting attributes:
- Center alignment
- 11-point Lucida Sans Bold
- Light Yellow fill color

5 Apply the Headings style to the remaining column headings in the worksheet.
6 Create another style named Costumes that will apply the following formatting attributes:
- 11-point Century Gothic
- Light Green fill color

7 Apply the Costumes style to the rows below the headings.
8 Change the font and font size for the text in rows 8 and 9. You determine the font and size.
9 Save Excel S4-P2.
10 Save Excel S4-P2 as a Web page and name it Costume Schedule.
11 View the Web page in the default browser and then close the window.
12 Print and then close Costume Schedule.

Activity 3: USING AUTOFILTER

1 Bobbie Sinclair, business manager at Performance Threads, needs a list of costumes for Marquee Productions that have a final delivery date of July 5. You decide to create the list using AutoFilter.
2 Open PT Costume Schedule.
3 Save the workbook in the *Excel Section 4* folder and name it Excel S4-P3.
4 Select A11:H16.
5 Turn on the AutoFilter feature and then deselect the range.
6 Use the AutoFilter button in column H to list only those costumes with a delivery date of July 5.
7 Change the page orientation to landscape and then print the filtered list.
8 Redisplay all of the data in the worksheet.
9 Turn off AutoFilter.
10 Save and then close Excel S4-P3.

Activity 4: INSERTING COMMENTS

1 The design team for the Marquee Productions costumes is meeting at the end of the week to discuss the production schedule. In preparation for this meeting, Bobbie Sinclair, business manager at Performance Threads, has asked you to review the schedule and send a revised worksheet with your comments inserted.
2 Open PT Costume Schedule.
3 Save the workbook in the *Excel Section 4* folder and name it Excel S4-P4.
4 Make D12 the active cell and then create the following comment:

Sue is working on the research for this costume and says she may not be finished in time for design to start on June 10.

5 Make D15 the active cell and then create the following comment:

This costume is the most complex in this project and it is also the earliest final delivery date. These dates may need adjustment.

6 Change the page orientation to landscape.

7 Display the Page Setup dialog box with the Sheet tab selected and then change the Comments option to *As displayed on sheet*.
8 Print Excel S4-P4.
9 Save and then close Excel S4-P4.

Activity 5: FINDING INFORMATION ON CREATING A TEMPLATE

1 Use Excel's Help feature to find information on creating your own template. Print the Help topic that you find with the steps displayed on saving a template.
2 Open Excel S4-R3.
3 Clear the contents of the following ranges:
   • B2
   • B4:H5
   • B7:H8
   • B10:H11

4 Save the revised worksheet as a template in the *Excel Section 4* folder and name it Weekly Sales Report.
5 Close Weekly Sales Report.
6 Open Weekly Sales Report and then key the following data:

B2	**22/02/2003**	B8	**109.00**
B4	**995.00**	B10	**219.00**
B5	**566.00**	B11	**134.00**
B7	**112.00**		

7 Save the workbook and name it Excel S4-P5. *(Note: Be sure to change the Save as type back to* Microsoft Excel Workbook (*.xls).*)*
8 Change the page orientation to landscape.
9 Print and then close Excel S4-P5.

Activity 6: FINDING FINANCIAL DATA FOR A CORPORATION

1 You are seeking employment with a large Canadian or U.S. corporation. You decide to use the Internet to locate financial data such as sales and profits for at least three corporations to determine where to target your resumes. (Most corporations that have stocks listed on the New York Stock Exchange, the Toronto Stock Exchange, or the Vancouver Stock Exchange will have recent financial data posted on their Web site.)
2 Create an Excel workbook that summarizes the financial data you were able to find, using a separate worksheet for each corporation. Include the dates that the data represents and a hyperlink to the Web addresses that you used.
3 Apply formatting enhancements to the worksheets.
4 Create a summary worksheet that lists each corporation you researched and links a cell in the summary worksheet to the sales value in the related worksheet.
5 Create a footer on all of the worksheets that prints your name at the bottom left margin and the current date at the right margin.
6 Save the workbook in the *Excel Section 4* folder and name it Excel S4-P6.
7 Print the entire workbook.
8 Close Excel S4-P6.

Integrating Word and Excel

A variety of methods are available for copying and pasting data and objects between Office programs. An object can be a table, workbook, chart, picture, text, or any other type of information you create. You can copy an object in one program and paste it into another or you can copy and link an object or copy and embed an object. The program containing the object is called the *source* program and the program containing the pasted, linked, or embedded object is called the *destination* program. When an object is linked, the object exists in the source program but not as a separate object in the destination program. Changes made to the object in the source program are automatically reflected in the object in the destination program. An embedded object resides in both the source and destination programs. You can edit an embedded object in the destination program using the tools of the source program. Deciding whether to copy and paste, copy and link, or copy and embed depends on how the information in the object is used. In this section you will learn the skills and complete the projects described here.

Skills

- Copy and paste Word data into an Excel worksheet
- Link an Excel worksheet with a Word document
- Update linked data
- View linked data as an icon
- Link an Excel chart with a Word document
- Embed an Excel worksheet into a Word document
- Edit an embedded worksheet

 Note: Before beginning this section, copy to a floppy disk or other folder the Integrated 01 *subfolder from the* Integrated *folder on the CD that accompanies this textbook, and then make* Integrated 01 *the active folder.*

Projects

 Copy data in a Word document on costume research, design, and sewing hours for employees into an Excel worksheet; copy data in an Excel worksheet on employee payroll and then link the data to a Word document; update the payroll hours for the employees for the next week; copy employee payroll data in an Excel worksheet to a Word document and then update the data in Word.

 Link a chart containing sales commissions for agents with a Word document and then update the sales commissions to reflect a higher percentage.

 Copy Word data on student scores into an Excel worksheet; copy an Excel chart containing data on student areas of emphasis in the Theatre Arts Division into a Word document and then update the chart in Excel.

Copy data in an Excel worksheet on theatre company revenues into a Word document and then update the data in Word.

I-1.1 Copying and Pasting Word Data into an Excel Worksheet

Microsoft Office is a suite that allows integration, which is the combining of data from two or more programs into one document. Integration can occur by copying and pasting data between programs. The program containing the data to be copied is called the *source* program and the program where the data is pasted is called the *destination* program. For example, you can copy data from a Word document into an Excel worksheet. Copy and paste data between programs in the same manner as you would copy and paste data within a program.

PROJECT: Copy data on costume research, design, and sewing hours for Performance Threads and paste the data into an Excel worksheet.

STEPS

1. Open Word and then open the document named PT Word Hours.

2. Open Excel and then open PT Excel Hours.

3. Save the worksheet with Save As and name it Int E1-01.

4. Click the button on the Taskbar representing the Word document PT Word Hours.

5. Select the five lines of text in columns as shown below.

6. Click the Copy button 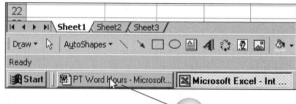 on the Standard toolbar.

Step 4

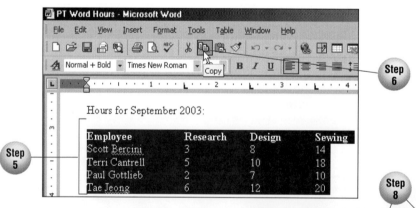

Hours for September 2003:

Employee	Research	Design	Sewing
Scott Bercini	3	8	14
Terri Cantrell	5	10	18
Paul Gottlieb	2	7	10
Tae Jeong	6	12	20

Step 5

Step 6

7. Click the button on the Taskbar representing the Excel document Int E1-01.

8. Make sure cell A11 is the active cell and then click the Paste button on the Standard toolbar.

Step 8

9. Make cell E11 the active cell, click the Bold button, and then key **Total**.

10. Make cell E12 the active cell, click the AutoSum button on the Standard toolbar, and then press Enter.

> This inserts a formula that calculates the total number of hours for Scott Bercini.

11. Copy the formula down to cells E13 through E15.

12. Make cell A16 the active cell, click the Bold button, and then key **Total**.

13. Make cell B16 the active cell, click the AutoSum button on the Standard toolbar, and then press Enter.

> This inserts a formula that calculates the total number of research hours.

14. Copy the formula in cell B16 to cells C16 through E16.

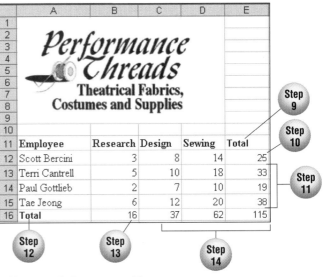

PROBLEM?

> If the results of your formula do not match what you see in the image, check your formula.

15. Select cells A11 through E16 and then apply an autoformat of your choosing.

16. Make any other changes needed to improve the visual display of the data in cells A11 through E16.

17. Save, print, and then close Int E1-01.

18. Click the button on the Taskbar representing the Word document PT Word Hours.

19. Close PT Word Hours.

In Addition

Cycling between Open Programs

Cycle through open programs by clicking the button on the Taskbar representing the desired program. You can also cycle through open programs by pressing Alt + Tab. Pressing Alt + Tab causes a menu to display. Continue holding down the Alt key and pressing the Tab key until the desired program icon is selected by a border in the menu and then release the Tab key and the Alt key.

IN BRIEF

Copy Data from One Program to Another
1. Open desired programs and documents.
2. Select data in source program.
3. Click Copy button.
4. Click button on Taskbar representing destination program.
5. Click Paste button.

I-1.2 Linking an Excel Worksheet with a Word Document

In the previous section, you copied data from a Word document and pasted it into an Excel worksheet. If you continuously update the data in the Word document, you would need to copy and paste the data each time into the Excel worksheet. If you update data on a regular basis that is copied to other programs, consider copying and linking the data. When data is linked, the data exists in the source program but not as separate data in the destination program. The destination program contains only a code that identifies the name and location of the source program, document, and the location in the document. Since the data is located only in the source program, changes made to the data in the source program are reflected in the destination program. Office updates a link automatically whenever you open the destination program or you edit the linked data in the destination program.

PROJECT: Copy data in an Excel worksheet on employee payroll for Performance Threads and then link the data to a Word document.

STEPS

1. With Word open and the active program, open the document named PT Word Oct Payroll.

2. Save the document with Save As and name it Int W1-01.

3. Make Excel the active program and then open the worksheet named PT Excel Oct Payroll.

4. Save the worksheet with Save As and name it Int E1-02.

5. Link the data in cells A13 through D18 into the Word document by selecting cells A13 through D18.

6. With the cells selected, click the Copy button [icon] on the Standard toolbar.

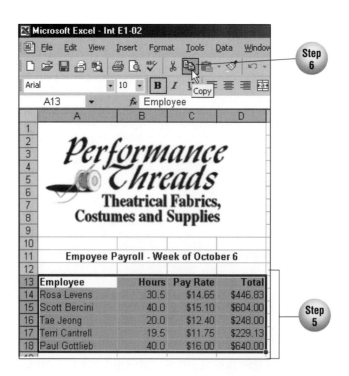

7 Click the button on the Taskbar representing the Word document Int W1-01.

8 Press Ctrl + End to move the insertion point to the end of the document (the insertion point is positioned a double space below *Week of October 6, 2003*).

9 Click Edit on the Menu bar and then click Paste Special.

10 At the Paste Special dialog box, click *Microsoft Excel Worksheet Object* in the As list box.

11 Click the Paste link option located at the left side of the dialog box.

12 Click OK to close the dialog box.

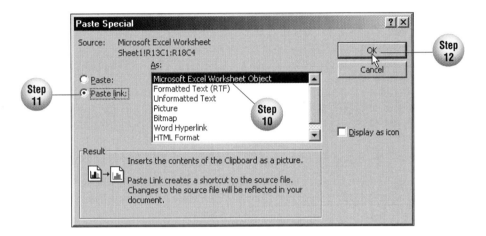

13 Save, print, and then close Int W1-01.

> The table gridlines do not print.

14 Click the button on the Taskbar representing the Excel worksheet Int E1-02.

15 Press the Esc key on the keyboard to remove the moving marquee around cells A13 through D18 and then click cell A10 to make it the active cell.

16 Save, print, and then close Int E1-02.

In Addition

Linking Data within a Program

Linking does not have to be between two different programs—data can be linked between documents in the same program. For example, you can create an object in a Word document such as a table or chart, and then link the object with another Word document (or several Word documents). If a change is made to the object in the original document, the linked object in the other document (or documents) is automatically updated.

IN BRIEF

Link Data between Programs
1 Open desired programs and documents.
2 Select data in source program.
3 Click Copy button.
4 Click button on Taskbar representing destination program.
5 Click Edit, Paste Special.
6 Click object in the As list box.
7 Click Paste link.
8 Click OK.

I-1.3 Updating Linked Data; Viewing a Link

The advantage of linking data over copying data is that editing the data in the source program will automatically update the data in the destination program. To edit linked data, open the document in the source program, make the desired edits, and then save the document. The next time you open the document in the destination program, the data is updated. The display of the linked data in the

destination program can be changed to an icon. The icon represents the document and program to which the object is linked.

PROJECT: Update the payroll hours for the employees of Performance Threads in the Excel worksheet for the week of October 13.

STEPS

1 Make Excel the active program and then open Int E1-02.

2 Make cell B14 the active cell and then change the number to *20.0*.

> Cells D14 through D18 contain a formula that multiplies the number in the cell in column B with the number in the cell in column C.

3 Make cell B16 the active cell and then change the number to *25.5*.

> When you make cell B16 the active cell, the result of the formula in cell D14 is updated to reflect the change you made to the number in cell B14.

4 Make cell B17 the active cell and then change the number to *15.0*.

5 Make cell C17 the active cell and then change the pay rate to *12.00*.

6 Double-click cell A11 and then change the date from *October 6* to *October 13*.

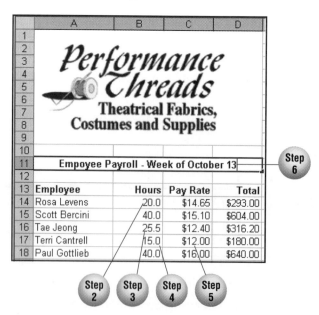

7 Save Int E1-02.

8 Print and then close Int E1-02.

9 Make Word the active program and then open Int W1-01.

> When you open the document, the table is automatically updated to reflect the changes you made in Int E1-02.

10. Change the date above the table from *October 6* to *October 13*.

11. Save and then print Int W1-01.

12. Display the linked table as an icon by clicking once on the table to select it (sizing handles display around the table). Click Edit, point to Linked Worksheet Object, and then click Convert.

13. At the Convert dialog box, click in the Display as icon check box to insert a check mark, and then click OK.

    Notice how the table is changed to an icon representing the linked document.

14. Print Int W1-01.

15. Make sure the linked object icon is still selected and then redisplay the table by clicking Edit, pointing to Linked Worksheet Object, and then clicking Convert.

16. At the Convert dialog box, click the Display as icon check box to remove the check mark, and then click OK.

17. Save and then close Int W1-01.

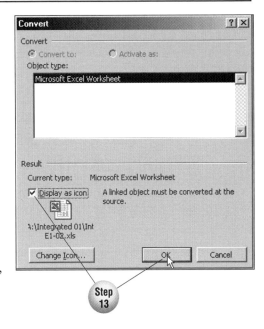

In Addition

Breaking a Link

The link between an object in the destination and source program can be broken. To break a link, select the object, click Edit, and then click Links. At the Links dialog box shown at the right, click the Break Link button. At the question asking if you are sure you want to break the link, click the Yes button.

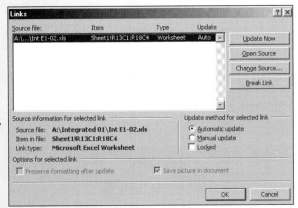

IN BRIEF

Update Linked Data
1. Open document in source program.
2. Made desired edits.
3. Save and close document.
4. Open document in destination program.
5. Save and close document.

Display Linked Object as an Icon
1. Select object.
2. Click Edit, point to Linked Worksheet Object, then click Convert.
3. At the Convert dialog box, click the Display as icon check box to insert a check mark.
4. Click OK.

I-1.4 Linking an Excel Chart with a Word Document

While a worksheet does an adequate job of representing data, you can present some data more visually by charting the data. A chart is a visual representation of numeric data and, like a worksheet, can be linked to a document in another program. Link a chart in the same manner as you would link a worksheet.

PROJECT: Link a chart containing sales commissions for agents of First Choice Travel with a Word document. Change the sales commission in the worksheet chart from 3 percent to 4 percent.

STEPS

1. Make Word the active program and then open FCT Word Sales Com.

2. Save the document with Save As and name it Int W1-02.

3. Make Excel the active program and then open FCT Excel Sales Com.

4. Save the worksheet with Save As and name it Int E1-03.

5. Click once in the chart area to select it (black sizing handles display around the chart).

   Make sure you do not select a specific chart element.

PROBLEM?

If you select a chart element, click outside the chart to deselect the element, and then try selecting the chart again.

6. Click the Copy button on the Standard toolbar.

7. Click the button on the Taskbar representing the Word document Int W1-02.

8. Press Ctrl + End to move the insertion point to the end of the document and then link the chart by clicking Edit and then Paste Special.

9. At the Paste Special dialog box, make sure *Microsoft Excel Chart Object* displays in the As list box, click Paste link, and then click OK.

10. Click outside the chart to deselect it.

11. Save and then print Int W1-02.

12. Click the button on the Taskbar representing the Excel worksheet Int E1-03.

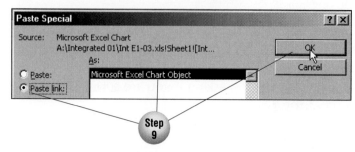

⑬ The chart is based on a sales commission of 3 percent. Change the formula so it calculates a sales commission of 4 percent by double-clicking in cell C5 and then changing the *3* in the formula to a *4*.

⑭ Press the Enter key.

> Pressing Enter displays the result of the formula calculating commissions at 4 percent.

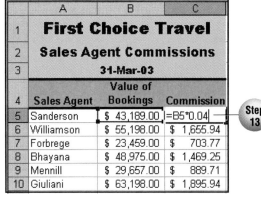

⑮ Make cell C5 the active cell and then copy the new formula down to cells C6 through C10.

⑯ Save and then close Int E1-03.

⑰ Click the button on the Taskbar representing the Word document Int W1-02.

> Notice the change in the amounts in the chart.

⑱ Save, print, and then close Int W1-02.

Step 15

	A	B	C
1	**First Choice Travel**		
2	**Sales Agent Commissions**		
3	**31-Mar-03**		
4	**Sales Agent**	**Value of Bookings**	**Commission**
5	Sanderson	$ 43,189.00	$ 1,727.56
6	Williamson	$ 55,198.00	$ 2,207.92
7	Forbrege	$ 23,459.00	$ 938.36
8	Bhayana	$ 48,975.00	$ 1,959.00
9	Mennill	$ 29,657.00	$ 1,186.28
10	Giuliani	$ 63,198.00	$ 2,527.92
11			
12			

In Addition

Customizing a Link

By default, a linked object is updated automatically and a linked object can be edited. You can change these defaults with options at the Links dialog box. If you want to control when to update linked data, click the Manual option located at the bottom of the Links dialog box. With the Manual option selected, update linked objects by clicking the Update Now button at the right side of the Links dialog box. If you do not want a linked object updated, click the Locked option at the Links dialog box.

I-1.5 Embedding an Excel Worksheet into a Word Document

An object can be copied between documents in a program, an object can be linked, and an object also can be embedded. A linked object resides in the source program, but not as a separate object in the destination program. An embedded object resides in the document in the source program as well as the destination program. If a change is made to an embedded object at the source program, the change is not made to the object in the destination program. Since an embedded object is not automatically updated as is a linked object, the only advantage to embedding rather than simply copying and pasting is that you can edit an embedded object in the destination program using the tools of the source program.

PROJECT: Copy data in an Excel worksheet on employee payroll for Performance Threads and then embed the data in a Word document.

STEPS

1. With Word open and the active program, open the document named PT Word Oct Payroll.

2. Save the document with Save As and name it Int W1-03.

3. Make Excel the active program and then open the worksheet named PT Excel Oct Payroll.

4. Save the worksheet with Save As and name it Int E1-04.

5. Embed the data in cells A13 through D18 into the Word document by selecting cells A13 through D18.

6. With the cells selected, click the Copy button ![Copy button] on the Standard toolbar.

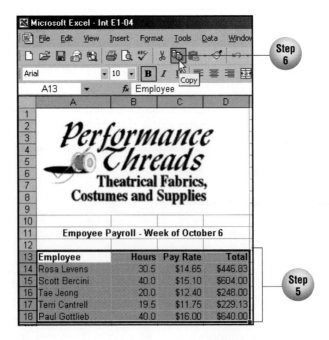

(7) Click the button on the Taskbar representing the Word document Int W1-03.

(8) Press Ctrl + End to move the insertion point to the end of the document (the insertion point is positioned a double space below *Week of October 6, 2003*).

(9) Click Edit on the Menu bar and then click Paste Special.

(10) At the Paste Special dialog box, click *Microsoft Excel Worksheet Object* in the As list box, and then click OK.

Make sure you do not click the Paste link option.

PROBLEM

(11) Click outside the table to deselect it.

(12) Save, print, and then close Int W1-03.

(13) Click the button on the Taskbar representing the Excel worksheet Int E1-04.

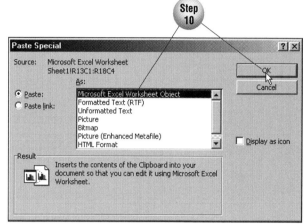

Step 10

(14) Press the Esc key to remove the moving marquee around cells A13 through D18.

(15) Click in cell A10 to make it the active cell.

(16) Save and then close Int E1-04.

In Addition

Inserting an Embedded Object from an Existing File

You embedded an Excel worksheet in a Word document using the Copy button and options at the Paste Special dialog box. Another method is available for embedding an object from an existing file. In the source program document, position the insertion point where you want the object embedded, then click Insert and then Object. At the Object dialog box, click the Create from File tab. At the Object dialog box with the Create from File tab selected, as shown at the right, key the desired file name in the File name text box or click the Browse button and then select the desired file from the appropriate folder. At the Object dialog box, make sure there is no check mark in the Link to file check box, and then click OK.

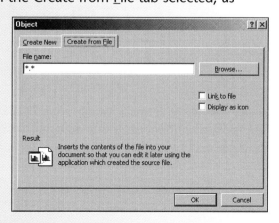

In Brief

Embed Data
1 Open desired programs and documents.
2 Select data in source program.
3 Click Copy button.
4 Click button on Taskbar representing destination program.
5 Click Edit, Paste Special.
6 Click object in the As list box.
7 Click OK.

I-1.6 Editing an Embedded Worksheet

An embedded object can be edited in the destination program using the tools of the source program. Double-click the object in the document in the destination program and the tools from the source program display. For example, if you double-click an Excel worksheet that is embedded in a Word document, the Excel Menu bar and Standard and Formatting toolbars display at the top of the screen.

PROJECT: Update the payroll hours for the employees of Performance Threads for the week of October 20 in the embedded Excel worksheet.

STEPS

1. With Word the active program, open Int W1-03.

2. Save the document with Save As and name it Int W1-04.

3. Change the date above the table from *October 6* to *October 20*.

4. Position the arrow pointer anywhere in the worksheet and then double-click the left mouse button.

   In a few moments, the worksheet displays surrounded by column and row designations and the Excel Menu bar, Standard toolbar, and Formatting toolbar display at the top of the screen.

5. To produce the ordered costumes on time, the part-time employees worked a full 40 hours for the week of October 20. Make cell B14 the active cell and then change the number to *40*.

6. Make cell B16 the active cell and then change the number to *40*.

7. Make cell B17 the active cell and then change the number to *40*.

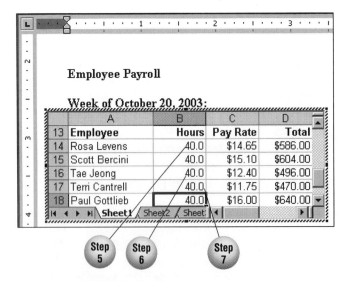

Employee Payroll

Week of October 20, 2003:

	A	B	C	D
13	Employee	Hours	Pay Rate	Total
14	Rosa Levens	40.0	$14.65	$586.00
15	Scott Bercini	40.0	$15.10	$604.00
16	Tae Jeong	40.0	$12.40	$496.00
17	Terri Cantrell	40.0	$11.75	$470.00
18	Paul Gottlieb	40.0	$16.00	$640.00

Step 5   Step 6   Step 7

8. Bobbie Sinclair, business manager, wants to know the payroll total for the week of October 20 to determine the impact it has on the monthly budget. Add a new row to the table by making cell A18 the active cell and then pressing the Enter key.

9. With cell A19 the active cell, key **Total**.

10   Make cell D19 the active cell and then click the AutoSum button Σ on the Standard toolbar.

11   Make sure *D14:D18* displays in cell D19 and then press the Enter key.

12   Increase the height of the worksheet by one row by positioning the arrow pointer on the bottom, middle black sizing square until the pointer turns into a double-headed arrow pointing up and down. Hold down the left mouse button, drag down one row, and then release the mouse button.

13   Using the arrow keys on the keyboard, make cell A13 the active cell and position cell A13 in the upper left corner of the worksheet. (This will display all cells in the worksheet containing data.)

14   Click outside the worksheet to deselect it.

15   Save, print, and then close Int W1-04.

      The gridlines do not print.

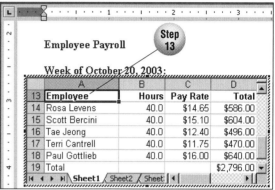

Step 13

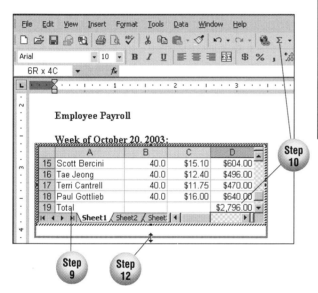

Step 10

Step 9   Step 12

In Addition

Troubleshooting Linking and Embedding Problems

If you double-click a linked or embedded object and a message appears telling you that the source file or source program cannot be opened, consider the following troubleshooting options. Check to make sure that the source program is installed on your computer. If the source program is not installed, convert the object to the file format of a program that is installed. Try closing other programs to free memory and make sure you have enough memory to run the source program. Check to make sure the source program does not have any dialog boxes open and, if it is a linked object, check to make sure someone else is not working in the source file.

In BRIEF

Edit an Embedded Object
1 In source program, double-click the embedded object.
2 Make desired edits.
3 Click outside the object.

SKILLS REVIEW

Activity 1: COPYING AND PASTING DATA

1   With Word the active program, open the document named NPC Word Scores.
2   Make Excel the active program and then open NPC Excel Scores.
3   Save the worksheet with Save As and name it Int E1-R1.
4   Click the button on the Taskbar representing the Word document NPC Word Scores.
5   Select the nine lines of text in columns (the line beginning *Student* through the line beginning *Yiu, Terry*) and then click the Copy button on the Standard toolbar.
6   Click the button on the Taskbar representing the Excel document Int E1-R1.
7   With cell A16 the active cell, paste the text into the worksheet.
8   Insert the text *Average* in cell E16.
9   Make cell E17 the active cell and then insert a formula that averages the numbers in cells B17 through D17.
10   Copy the formula in cell E17 down to cells E18 through E24.
11   Select cells E17 through E24, change the font to 12-point Tahoma, and then click the Decrease Decimal button three times.
12   Select cells B17 through D24 and then click once on the Increase Decimal button on the Formatting toolbar. (This displays two numbers after the decimal point.)
13   With cells B17 through E24 still selected, click the Center button on the Formatting toolbar, and then deselect the cells.
14   Save, print, and then close Int E1-R1.
15   Click the button on the Taskbar representing the Word document NPC Word Scores and then close NPC Word Scores.

Activity 2: LINKING AN OBJECT

1   With Word the active program, open the document named NPC Word Enrollment.
2   Save the document with Save As and name it Int W1-R1.
3   Make Excel the active program and then open the worksheet named NPC Excel Chart.
4   Save the worksheet with Save As and name it Int E1-R2.
5   Link the chart to the Word document Int W1-R1 a triple space below the *Student Enrollment* subtitle. (Make sure you use the Paste Special dialog box.)
6   Center the chart below the subtitle *Student Enrollment*.
7   Save, print, and close Int W1-R1.
8   Click the button on the Taskbar representing Int E1-R2.
9   Press the Esc key to remove the moving marquee and then click outside the chart to deselect it.
10   Save, print, and then close Int E1-R2.

Activity 3: EDITING A LINKED OBJECT

1 With Excel the active program, open Int E1-R2.
2 Make the following changes to the data in the specified cells:

    A10   =   Change *Fall Term* to *Spring Term*
    B12   =   Change *75* to *98*
    B13   =   Change *30* to *25*
    B14   =   Change *15* to *23*
    B15   =   Change *38* to *52*
    B16   =   Change *25* to *10*

3 Make cell A9 active.
4 Save, print, and then close Int E1-R2.
5 Make Word the active program and then open Int W1-R1.
6 Save, print, and then close Int W1-R1.

Activity 4: EMBEDDING AN OBJECT

1 With Word the active program, open the document named WE Revenues Memo.
2 Save the document with Save As and name it Int W1-R2.
3 Make Excel the active program and then open the worksheet named WE Excel Revenues.
4 Save the worksheet with Save As and name it Int E1-R3.
5 Embed the data in cells A13 through D19 to the Word document Int W1-R2 a double space below the paragraph of text in the body of the memo.
6 Save, print, and then close Int W1-R2.
7 Click the button on the Taskbar representing Int E1-R3.
8 Press the Esc key to remove the moving marquee and then click outside the selected cells.
9 Save, print, and then close Int E1-R3.

Activity 5: EDITING AN EMBEDDED OBJECT

1 Make Word the active program and then open Int W1-R2.
2 Save the document with Save As and name it Int W1-R3.
3 Double-click the worksheet and then make the following changes to the data in the specified cells:

    A13   =   Change *July Revenues* to *August Revenues*
    B15   =   Change *1,356,000* to *1,575,000*
    B16   =   Change *2,450,000* to *2,375,000*
    B17   =   Change *1,635,000* to *1,750,000*
    B18   =   Change *950,000* to *1,100,000*
    B19   =   Change *1,050,000* to *1,255,000*

4 Click outside the worksheet to deselect it.
5 Save, print, and then close Int W1-R3.